The Welsh Peaks

Books on Wales by the same author

SNOWDONIA THROUGH THE LENS

SNOWDON HOLIDAY

WANDERINGS IN WALES

ESCAPE TO THE HILLS – PART ONLY

Companions to this volume

THE LAKELAND PEAKS

THE SCOTTISH PEAKS

THE PEAK & PENNINES

Plate 1 **Route 18**—Tryfan in winter raiment

W. A. Poucher Hon. F.R.P.S.

The Welsh Peaks

A Pictorial Guide to walking in this region
and to the safe ascent of its principal mountain groups

with 250 photographs by the author
15 Maps and 56 Routes

Seventh Edition

Constable London

First published in Great Britain 1962
by Constable and Company Ltd
10 Orange Street London WC2H 7EG

Second edition 1965
Third edition 1967
Fourth edition 1970
Fifth edition 1973
Sixth edition 1977
Seventh edition 1979

ISBN 0 09 463180 8

Set in Monophoto Times New Roman 9pt
Filmset and printed in Great Britain by
BAS Printers Limited, Wallop, Hampshire

The author is a member of
The Climbers' Club
The Fell & Rock Climbing Club

Preface to the seventh edition

Readers will be interested to know that a Snowdon Management Scheme has been launched that will take five years to complete. Its main objectives are the restoration, improvement and maintenance of the summit and the eroded paths that rise to it, together with the establishment, extension and landscaping of the car parks in the Llanberis Pass. This will be welcomed by nearly half a million visitors who come to enjoy the superlative beauty of this mountain every year.

Erosion of some of the routes to Snowdon has posed many difficult problems, and particularly so that of the Zig-Zags on the Pyg Track. This has already been admirably dealt with by the Warden Service as noted in Route 2, and the final section of Routes 4 and 5, from Bwlch Saethau to the summit, still needs care in both ascent and descent. They have also rendered a great service to the climber by erecting one monolith on Bwlch Glas at the exact point where the Zig-Zags leave the ridge, an invaluable indication in bad weather, another beside the railway track where the Snowdon Ranger begins the true descent and a similar monolith between Bwlch Main and the summit where the Watkin Path leaves the ridge and intersects the Rhyd Ddu path.

Cairns are an invaluable indication of a route in bad weather, and especially so in mist, but in the Welsh Peaks most of the paths have been made to a standard which minimise erosion and at the same time maintain direction. And furthermore, if any intersection or change of direction is made in the track, then a monolith has been erected to indicate it. But, strange as it may seem, a new sport has been evolved by thoughtless walkers who build additional cairns themselves, using the stone from the surface of the path and therefore accelerating erosion. Will readers please take a special note of this crazy idea and should they encounter anyone doing so, immediately put a stop to it.

Access problems have arisen recently in the descent of Moel Siabod, where walkers have deserted the route of ascent, taken short cuts across enclosed land and brought down fences and walls. It will help if the two routes herein are strictly adhered to by everyone.

And here I would like to pay tribute to John Ellis Roberts, the Head Warden of the Snowdonia National Park, who knows these hills like the back of his hand, and since 1974 has not only taken part in over 300 mountain rescue operations, but has also directed the work of his staff to the improvement of every feature in this delectable countryside.

A question that is frequently posed to me is "What cameras do you use?" Well, there is no reason why I should not divulge this seeming secret in print, so I will say that since the availability of 35 mm film I have always used Leicas, and replaced them as new models appeared. I have now two M2s (one of them in case of accident), with 35 mm wide angle, 50 mm normal and 90 mm long focus lenses. These I use for monochrome and my favourite film is Kodak Plus X. I also have a Leicaflex with 28 mm wide angle, 50 mm normal, 90 mm long focus and 135 mm telephoto lenses. I use them exclusively for colour and my favourite film is Kodachrome 25.

In view of the vast scope of this book it is obviously impossible to check frequently every one of the descriptions of the routes. Time, usage, rock falls, erosion and local weather may be responsible for slight variations and should any reader encounter any inaccuracy I would appreciate a note of it for inclusion in future editions of this work.

It should be noted that the Routes described and illustrated herein have been frequented over the years without objection, but they do not necessarily constitute a Right of Way. If in doubt, the reader should contact the owner of the land and ask permission to cross it before embarking upon his walk. This is most important in view of the scourge of vandalism now sweeping the country, which has resulted in damage to fences, hedges, gates, walls, cairns and shelters in mountainous districts; which is not only deplorable but also contrary to the accepted Country Code.

Finally, I would urge Leaders of school and youth parties not to venture on these hills unless the weather is favourable, and moreover, they should always insist upon everyone wearing boots and proper clothing. For, by doing so they will not only reduce the risk of accidents, but also avoid the often needless call for Mountain Rescue.

A suggestion for a ROUTE CARD appears at the end of this volume and its use by every walker and climber could help to reduce the number of casualties on our peaks. Please report your route to your lodgings and do not deviate from it. I am glad to say it has been adopted in Snowdonia.

The fifteen maps are reproduced with the permission of John Bartholomew & Son Limited.

W. A. Poucher
4 Heathfield
Reigate Heath Surrey

Contents

Introductory notes

The coastal resorts of Wales have been a treasured venue for the holidaymaker for many decades, and with the increased interest in mountain walking and rock climbing Snowdonia too has achieved an immense popularity that is second to none in this country. But the remote and wild landscape of South and Mid-Wales has for some inexplicable reason escaped this attention, despite the magnificence of the scenery, the opportunities for hill walking in comparative solitude, and the possibility of ascents of varying difficulty on its innumerable crags and cliffs. Today accessibility is no excuse for this neglect, because almost all the narrow winding roads leading into the hills have been either improved or resurfaced, and as cars are nowadays within the reach of almost everyone I hope the information given in these pages will lead to a more extensive exploration of the whole of the Principality.

At the present time most of our young people have ample funds available for holidays, and since youth hostelling and camping are an inexpensive form of travel there is no valid reason why this country as a whole should not become as cherished a centre as any other in Britain. Energetic young men and women who have a special predilection for hill country may well choose Snowdonia for their first visit, and on arrival they will raise their eyes to the peaks and imagine themselves standing by one of the summit cairns, inhaling the invigorating mountain air and scanning the valleys far below, the chain of engirdling hills and the distant glimmering seas. Come what may, they lose no time in setting out to climb one of them, and on reaching their objective gain that satisfaction that comes only after the ardours of the ascent. It is highly probable that Snowdon will be their first conquest, not only because it is the monarch of Wales and the countryside as far north as the border, but also because they believe it will disclose the finest and most comprehensive panorama on account of its dominating altitude. On achieving this ambition, they quite naturally speculate upon the merits of the views from the other high peaks in the region, and after talking over the question with friends they will in all probability continue their exploration by climbing Tryfan, or walking over the Glyders, or perhaps even traversing the fine Nantlle Ridge, on their first vacation.

On returning home they will often ponder over these experiences, and especially so if they have been captivated by the spirit and mystery of the hills. The map will doubtless be unfolded at frequent intervals, and by tracing the routes thereon they will re-live these happy times. If they climbed Snowdon by the Pyg Track, their thoughts will follow that pleasant route from Pen-y-pass with Crib Goch rising into the sky ahead, their surprise at the fine view of Lliwedd on attaining Bwlch y Moch, the tramp along the stony undulating path with Yr Wyddfa in front and the sudden appearance of Glaslyn below, the scramble up the steep Zig-Zags to the col where the Snowdon Railway first comes into view, the walk along the edge of the cwm with Snowdon ahead and the exhilaration of finally standing on the large cairn on the roof of Wales with a whole kingdom spread out far below.

A close inspection of the map will suggest to our friends several other routes to this lofty peak, and curiosity will induce them to speculate upon their respective merits. Would the Miners' Track have been more interesting? Perhaps it would have been more thrilling to have made the ascent from the beautiful Vale of Gwynant by the Watkin Path, or what of the more distant approaches from the Snowdon Ranger Youth Hostel or Rhyd-ddu? Then another line of thought may develop; for they had seen a grand array of peaks engirdling the horizon from Yr Wyddfa and they will speculate again upon the merits of the panoramas from their summits, to realise with surprise that a lifetime is not too long in which to become acquainted with them all.

The cogitations of our young friends will follow a normal

course and they will do exactly the same as the rest of us did in our novitiate; for they will formulate the plans for their next holiday long before it is due. Next time they may decide to stay perhaps in Mid-Wales and explore the adjacent hills; but which ones? To solve this problem they will often get out the map, and while scanning it with happy anticipation compare it with the various guide-books which describe this lovely countryside. There they will *read* what their authors have so lucidly written, but much will inevitably be left to their imagination.

It is here that my long experience of the Welsh Peaks will help them to solve their problems, for by consulting this volume in conjunction with my other works devoted to this region they will not only be able to choose their centre with certainty, their routes to the peaks in the vicinity in accordance with their powers as climbers, and their subjects for their cameras if they happen to be photographers, but they will also be able to *see* beforehand through the medium of my camera studies precisely the type of country that will satisfy every one of their needs.

Equipment

Anyone who ventures on the hills without proper equipment is asking for trouble, and since the weather is one of our greatest hazards it is wise, and indeed imperative, to be prepared for sudden changes, as for instance from warm sunshine to rain or blizzard, by wearing proper boots and clothing, as well as other relatively inexpensive but useful incidentals which I shall enumerate in these pages.

Boots are of course the most important item, and climbing boots are expensive, but those who can afford the best will be amply repaid by their comfort and service through years of tough wear. There are several patterns, and since I have already described and illustrated the best type of *nailed* boots in my *Lakeland Peaks*, I will not repeat the advice here because in recent years tastes have changed and I will therefore now deal only with Vibrams.

In the last decade there has been a standardisation of type, but a wide variety in design detail depending upon price and the use to which the boots will be put in the hills. And while there are many excellent British makes it is possible the Italians have concentrated more on a greater variety in design. Side stitching has been abandoned because of possible friction to the ankles, and instead replaced by two pieces of soft leather interspersed with padding and stitched only at the heel. The lacing goes up from the toe and is threaded through hooks and eyes so the user can adjust tightness or looseness as desired. The best thing to do is to inspect the different models in a good mountaineering shop and take the advice of the salesman after trying on those recommended.

There is a choice of rubber sole between Vibrams and Itshide Commandos, and the selection is a matter of taste. In addition, as further security for rock climbing, there are types

Plate 2

having No. 6 Tricouni round soles and heels, and even heel plates if preferred. There are advantages and disadvantages in rubber soles without these trimmings: they are silent and easier on the feet on DRY rock, but on WET rock or moss-covered slabs they can be a handicap to rapid progress because the utmost care becomes imperative to avoid a slip which in an exposed situation might result in a twisted or broken ankle. Strong laces are vital and there is a wide choice between nylon, waxed fabric, and leather.

Light weight boots are not usually acceptable to the climber, but a new one—the Sportkiker—has recently been made by Clarks, and after wearing a pair in Scotland for three weeks I can recommend them to those who confine their walking to smooth or stony tracks. The great advantage I found was that they could be worn while driving my Dolomite Sprint, step out of the car and walk straight up any grassy hill without having to change into climbing boots. The Contura moulded sole with its built in Arch Support is shaped to allow the toes to splay without friction, and the uppers are supple and comfortable round the ankles and the bellows water resistant tongue keeps the feet dry. This is the ideal Hiker's boot, but it does not possess the ankle support that is vital when climbing steep ground or rocky peaks.

Stockings and socks are worthy of some attention and one of each worn together ensure comfort and warmth and reduce undue friction. The *colour* of these items may be important and for some years I have worn RED because in case of accident this colour can be seen at a great distance, and in consequence would facilitate location and subsequent rescue.

Clothes are perhaps a matter of personal taste, and there are still a few climbers who delight in wearing their oldest cast-off suits, often intentionally with brilliant patches as a decoration! But there is more protection when wearing a properly made *Alpine Jacket*, of which there are a variety of patterns and colours and one of the smartest for summer wear in the hills is a Berghaus Alpen Lovat. They are usually made from closely woven cotton of double texture at the main points of friction. They are windproof and reasonably waterproof and perfectly so if treated with silicone or polyurethane. Good models have four pockets, of which two are large enough to accommodate maps which are then kept dry. A skirt is now made to all types, and in heavy rain keeps moisture from percolating on to the small of the back. The collar could be lined with wool to keep the neck warm in the absence of a scarf. In the better jackets there is a small zip opening below the back of the neck to accommodate the hood when not in use. Outside belts are no longer worn because they may put a rock climber off-balance by inadvertently catching on a tiny excrescence of crag. They are now universally replaced by a draw cord which runs in a groove at the waist between the double-texture cloth. This type of Alpine Jacket has a zip fastener down the front and goes well up into the neck, whereas *Anoraks* are made in one piece, with a large kangaroo pocket at breast height and a short zip only at the neck. Nylon is now replacing cotton in some models. For climbers who prefer a smart garment for wear in cold weather on the tops, I have found nothing better than a Pointfive High Sierra Jacket with double open ended zips, which is exceptionally light and warm. In very stormy weather a Gore-Tex Mistral gives the best protection as it keeps out the rain and allows the perspiration to evaporate through the material. In view of the rapid changes of temperature encountered in hill country, it is always advisable to carry spare *Pullovers*. Those made of light Shetland wool are much better than a heavy one, because the layers of warm air between them maintain the body temperature, and the number worn can be easily adjusted to varying conditions. *String Vests* worn next to the skin have reduced the risks of colds, and by their use the number of pullovers can be cut down considerably. *Leg Gear* is a matter of choice; some climbers swear by trousers while others prefer plus twos. Personally I consider the latter more comfortable and in addition they allow more freedom about the feet. The *material* from which they are made is another consideration. Many have a preference for corduroy, but I do not care for it because it is made of cotton and therefore acts like a sponge and retains an excess of moisture. The weight about the legs then increases and is attended by much discomfort. Alternatively, hard wearing and close-woven tweed is warm and light in weight and altogether more amenable in all mountain weather. *Headgear* has changed considerably in recent years, and the feathered, velour Austrian hat is seldom seen nowadays. The more practical and useful protection is at present confined to two types: the woollen brightly coloured *Bob-Cap* and the old-fashioned *Balaclava Helmet*. In fair weather the former functions admirably and will not blow off in a strong wind, whereas the latter is indispensable in Alpine conditions.

GORE-TEX is a micro porous film which is laminated between the inner and outer layers of fabric and promises to be of great value in mountaineering clothing. For, while the internal body vapour is allowed to escape, the wearer keeps dry and comfortable and at the same time is protected from rain and wind. Interested readers are respectfully referred to a complete account of it in the 7th edition of my *Lakeland Peaks*.

Rucksacks are a necessity and may be obtained in a variety of shapes, colours, sizes and weights. If the climber is moving from place to place and wishes to carry spare clothing, incidentals and photographic gadgets, then it must be a large one such as a Bergan or Karrimor, otherwise a small light model should give satisfactory service. Some prefer those having a light metal frame which keeps the sack off the back and so allows plenty of ventilation. In addition I have one with a leather base to both sack and pockets which increases its durability and prolongs its life.

Maps of this extensive region should be the guide and friend of all who climb the Welsh Peaks. There are two series of outstanding merit, and if dissected and mounted on linen they are more easily handled out of doors, but the present cost is so prohibitive that their general use is declining. The one-inch series issued by the Ordnance Survey up to 1974 had the contours at intervals of fifty feet, and the relevant sheets were as follows: No. 107, Snowdonia; No. 116, Cadair Idris, The Arans, the Arennigs and the Harlech Dome; No. 127, Plynlimon; and No. 141, the Black Mountains and the Brecon Beacons. But a new Second Series of revised maps at a scale of 1:50000, which is approximately $1\frac{1}{4}$ inches to the mile, now replaces the above sheets and the heights are in metres. However, this change will not necessitate any alterations to the Routes on the maps in this edition, although it may be desirable to change them when the metric system is generally adopted in this country. Four new Leisure Maps have recently been issued at a scale of 1 to 25,000. They cover most of Snowdonia and show the public rights of way, car parks, viewpoints etc. The half-inch series issued by Bartholomew have the contours at intervals of 250 feet, but the splendid layer system of colouring reveals the topography of the country with great clarity. The maps in this work are marked with the various routes to the peaks and should be of immense value to all climbers.

A compass should always be carried in the hills, despite the fact that it may not be needed in clear weather if the ground is familiar. In mist, however, all mountains become wrapped in deeper mystery with the complete disappearance of well-known landmarks, and if the climber is off the beaten track he may well find himself in difficulties without one. A good compass is not cheap, but it is money well spent. Mountain photographers should note that certain types of Exposure Meter containing a magnet may deflect the compass needle if the two are within a short distance of one another. Tests I have made indicate that at a distance of 9 inches N, 12 inches E, and 18 inches S and W the magnetic north is deflected, and when the exposure meter is close to the compass the needle simply spins round. Climbers should therefore test the two instruments and keep one well away from the other when in use, as in misty weather incorrect route finding might result and so lead to unforeseen difficulties.

An aneroid is a most useful instrument and may be a luxury to all save the explorer. A good one is a fairly reliable forecaster of the weather, and since it approximately indicates the altitude it may be a valuable aid in misty weather by helping to locate one's position with greater accuracy. The lower-priced instruments register up to a height of 10,000 feet. If you possess one, always remember to adjust the dial to the altitude of the starting point of your climb, if it is known with certainty, and thereafter check it at any known station. Bear in mind that when the barometer is falling the readings will be too high, and if it is rising they will be too low. In any event the error is about 100 feet for each 1/10 of an inch of rise or fall not due to change of altitude.

An ice axe is valuable and may be indispensable in snow climbing; moreover, it is a useful tool for glissading and its correct employment will ensure a safe and rapid descent of steep snow slopes. There are numerous makes, each of which has some slight variation in design of both pick and adze. A competent dealer will advise on the most suitable type, which is largely governed by length of shaft, weight and balance. A sling is a useful adjunct and may prevent the loss of the axe if it should slip out of the hand when in use.

In conclusion, I would advise everyone venturing on the hills at any time of year to carry the following items which could spell survival in extremely bad weather. (1) Map and compass; (2) torch and whistle; (3) spare food and clothing, including a large polythene bag; and (4) a small first aid kit.

Rock climbing

North Wales is resplendent with precipitous cliffs of sound rock that in recent years have become the treasured playground of the rock climber. Those of Clogwyn Du'r Arddu, Lliwedd, Craig yr Ysfa, Silyn, Llanberis Pass, Glyder Fach and Idwal afford courses of varying difficulty, and during the holiday season are much favoured by intrepid cragsmen. Courses in South and Mid-Wales are comparatively rare, but a few years ago climbers explored the buttresses and gullies of Craig Cywarch, in the Arans, and doubtless others will follow as interest increases in this sport.

There are thus ample opportunities for the enjoyment of this exhilarating pastime among the Welsh Peaks, but a novice should never attempt it without proper guidance and training. If you have a friend who is an experienced rock climber, ask him to explain its technique and the management of the rope, and at the first opportunity get him to lead you up some of the easy courses, when you will have the chance to put these theories into practice. If you have a steady head, good balance and can acquire the rhythm required for proficiency, he will soon notice it and lead you up routes of greater difficulty until finally you tackle the severes.

Should you become keen on this fascinating sport, you may wish to apply for membership of one of the clubs or associations whose activities are concentrated mainly in Wales. The following information may be helpful, but it should be borne in mind that some of the clubs are already full and unable to consider further applications for membership.

The Climbers' Club was formed in Snowdonia and its objects are to encourage mountaineering and hill walking, to further the interests of science and art in relation thereto, and to guard and promote the general interests of mountaineers.

All gentlemen, and now ladies, interested in the objects of the club, as defined above, are eligible as members. Candidates for admission must be proposed and seconded by members of not less than two years' standing, who must have personal knowledge of the candidate. There are three club huts in North Wales. Helyg is situated on the Holyhead Road, two and a half miles from Capel Curig; it is near Tryfan and gives easy access to its three fine buttresses. The R. W. Lloyd Hut, Ynys Etws, is situated in the Llanberis Pass, about one and a half miles above the bus terminus at Nant Peris. Cwm Glas Mawr is also in the Llanberis Pass near Blaen-y-nant Farm and about one mile up the valley from the same bus stop. *The Midland Association of Mountaineers* has its headquarters in Birmingham and owns Glandena, a conspicuous hut situated just above the headwaters of Llyn Ogwen and beside the Holyhead Road. *The Rucksack Club* is very active in Manchester and owns Beudy-mawr which is situated in the Llanberis Pass, two and a half miles below Pen-y-pass. Finally there is *Plas y Brenin*, the National Mountaineering Centre, administered by the Sports Council and situated just beside the twin Capel Lakes. The main purpose of the centre is to provide residential training in outdoor activities such as rock climbing, mountain walking, map and compass reading, mobile camping, etc. Other clubs, not primarily concerned with Wales, are the *Ramblers' Association* and the *Camping Club*, many of whose members are experienced mountaineers.

The Welsh centres

In the following list I have given the principal centres from which the Welsh Peaks may be most conveniently climbed. But it should be borne in mind that strong walkers are often able to reach them from more distant places, and remote Youth Hostels which are occasionally less conveniently situated. At the time of writing there were forty-five hostels in Wales, but I have only cited those giving reasonably easy access to the major hill ranges. Since this region is so vast, I have enumerated the centres under three well-defined mountain areas: Snowdonia, Mid-Wales and South Wales.

Snowdonia

Betws-y-coed is the Gateway to Snowdonia for perhaps the majority of visitors, and is well situated on the River Conway at an important road junction. It has also the advantage of a railway connection with Llandudno Junction on the main line from London and the Midlands. Most of the region can be explored by motorists from its many hotels, as one highway leads into the heart of the peaks and the other penetrates the sylvan stretches of the Lledr Valley. It is too far away to be a really convenient centre for the climber, but there is a Youth Hostel at Pont-y-pant on the way to Dolwyddelan.

Capel Curig is exceptionally well placed at the road junction to Llanberis and Bethesda and is an excellent centre for the climber. There are some comfortable hotels, several guest houses and a Youth Hostel. All the peaks are readily accessible to the motorist and buses serve many of them too. Moel Siabod rises almost overhead and the eastern tops of the Carneddau and Glyders are only a short step away.

Ogwen Cottage is situated at the foot of Llyn Ogwen and

on the crest of Nant Ffrancon. It stands in the very shadow of the peaks and affords easy access to the Carneddau, the Milestone Buttress, Tryfan, Idwal and the whole of the Glyders. But it is now a Mountain School, owned by the City of Birmingham, and has recently been much enlarged. Climbers desiring further information should write direct to the warden. There is a Youth Hostel nearby.

Bethesda is situated at the foot of Nant Ffrancon and has an hotel and several guest houses. It is too far away from the main peaks for the average pedestrian, but those who wish to be near the western Glyders and the south-western Carneddau will find it a good centre.

Pen-y-gwryd is perhaps the most famous climbers' centre in the whole of Snowdonia, and stands at the junction of the roads to Llanberis and Beddgelert. It is encircled by the lower slopes of Snowdon, the Glyders and Moel Siabod, and thus gives easy access to many of their peaks. The hotel has a long mountaineering history and will always be closely associated with the Climbers' and Pinnacle clubs.

Pen-y-pass is equally well known and is superbly situated on the lofty crest of the Llanberis Pass. It is the starting point for the Snowdon Horseshoe, for other favoured routes to Yr Wyddfa, for the direct ascent of Glyder Fawr and Esgair Felen, and gives easy access to Llyn Llydaw. The name of the distinguished mountaineer Geoffrey Winthrop Young will always be associated with it and also with his famous Easter parties. It is now a Youth Hostel and Restaurant and there is a large car park nearby.

Llanberis stands on the shore of Llyn Padarn at the foot of the Llanberis Pass and may be reached by bus from Caernarvon. It is the starting point of the Snowdon Railway, has several good hotels and guest houses, and there is a Youth Hostel on the mountainside above the town. It is the best centre for climbers making the long ascent to Yr Wyddfa by the well-trodden Llanberis Path, and also gives ready access to the frowning cliffs of Clogwyn Du'r Arddu.

Beddgelert spans the Afon Glaslyn at the junction of the main roads leading to Caernarvon, Portmadoc and Capel Curig and has several comfortable hotels and guest houses. The village is surrounded by the lower slopes of Snowdon and the southern satellites of Moel Siabod, while it is almost overshadowed by the fine peak of Moel Hebog. It is also within reasonable distance of Aberglaslyn Pass, and with the paths ascending the south side of Yr Wyddfa. The Nantlle Ridge is too far away for the average pedestrian, but may be reached by car or bus. Some four miles up the beautiful Vale of Gwynant stands the Youth Hostel of Bryn Gwynant, splendidly situated in a delightful sylvan setting overlooking the lake, while the guest house of the Holiday Fellowship is not far distant. Both are well placed for the ascent of Snowdon by the Watkin Path.

The Snowdon Ranger is now a Youth Hostel and is pleasantly situated on the shore of Llyn Cwellyn. The path to Yr Wyddfa, well known as the Snowdon Ranger, starts from its very door and may be the oldest route on this mountain. It is also well placed for access to the Nantlle Ridge and to Mynydd Mawr, which rises on the other side of the lake. It may be conveniently reached by bus from Caernarvon or Beddgelert. There is a small car park opposite the starting point.

Mid-Wales

Dolgellau, formerly known as Dolgelley, is centrally situated amid this vast area of peaks, which are so widely spread that those who stay here must use a car to reach them. It has one good hotel and there is a smaller one at Cross Foxes. The Youth Hostel of Kings is four miles away in the direction of Arthog. The town is well placed for the ascent of Cadair Idris by the famous Foxes' Path, for the rock traverse of the shattered ridge of Cyfrwy, and also gives easy access to the Precipice and Torrent Walks, two of the scenic gems in this district.

Tal-y-llyn is the most romantically situated centre in Mid-Wales, and its two small but comfortable hotels stand at the foot of a sequestered lake that is completely enclosed by hills. It is the ideal starting point for the ascent of Cadair Idris by way of Cwm y Cau, one of the wildest in the Principality, and also for the ascent of the Pencoed Pillar, a nice problem for the rock climber.

Dinas Mawddwy has one hotel and is the only convenient centre for pedestrians wishing to make the most interesting ascent of the Arans. The key to this walk is the hamlet of Abercywarch, a mile to the north of the town, whence Cae Peris is reached by a narrow and twisting farm road giving access not only to the path to the two peaks but also to Craig Cywarch, a little-known crag of interest to the rock climber. There is a hut nearby.

Bala occupies a splendid position at the northern extremity of Llyn Tegid, but its hotels and guest houses are rather distant from the Arans and Arennigs, although strong walkers may attain the summits of either group in a long day. Those who can find accommodation in one of the cottages in Llanuwchllyn, a village at the southern extremity of Bala Lake, will be better placed for the ascents of both ranges and especially so for Aran Benllyn, which is the nearer of the two.

Harlech is the nearest centre with adequate hotel accommodation and a Youth Hostel for those wishing to explore the Harlech Dome. A new one has recently been opened near Cwm Bychau at Gerddi Bluog. It is a rugged backbone of bare mountains in the hinterland, in which the Roman Steps and the Rhinogs afford the toughest and most attractive climbing. Those having a car at their disposal may drive along the road to Barmouth and turn off to the left at Llanbedr, whence narrow and twisting lanes give access to one or other of the starting points that will be indicated later in this volume.

Llanbedr is a better centre for pedestrians undertaking the above expeditions, and there is a small hotel in the village.

Barmouth is an attractive seaside resort lying at the base of the southern slopes of the Harlech Dome, but is too far distant for the ascent of these peaks unless a car can be used for the long approach. The local scenic highlight is the famous Panorama Walk, which reveals fine views of the Mawddach Estuary below, backed by the precipitous front of Cadair Idris.

The Devil's Bridge is some twelve miles to the east of Aberystwyth and has a splendidly situated hotel overlooking the deep wooded stretches of the Rheidol Valley, from which it may be conveniently explored. It is a good though distant centre for the ascent of Plynlimon, when transport is desirable to reach the starting points of this walk. But pedestrians may secure accommodation at the Duffryn Castell Inn which lies at the foot of this immense sprawling mountain and the well-marked track to its summit is three and a half miles in length. Accommodation may also be found at Eisteddfa Gurig for the shorter route of ascent and there is a good hotel in Ponterwyd and a Youth Hostel at Ystumtuen.

South Wales

Abergavenny has two hotels and is a convenient centre for motorists who wish to penetrate the deep valleys of the Black Mountains. Their bare, whaleback ridges afford excellent walking country some miles to the north of the town. There is a Youth Hostel at Capel-y-ffin.

Crickhowell also has two hotels, and some motorists may prefer to stay here for these pleasant drives. There is a Youth Hostel in the town.

Talgarth has one hotel and is the nearest town to the lofty Gadair Ridge which dominates the Black Mountains. Its crest may be most easily attained from the tiny adjacent hamlet of Pen-y-genffordd.

Hay lies in the Wye Valley to the north of the range and has two small hotels which are rather distant for the average pedestrian.

Brecon is the only centre with hotel accommodation near the Brecon Beacons, and a car is useful for those who wish to make the complete traverse of the lofty ridge that is dominated by Pen y Fan, the most picturesque peak in this range. There is a Youth Hostel at Ty'n-y-caeau, some two and a half miles to the east of the town.

Storey Arms is the nearest starting point for Pen y Fan and eight and a half miles from Brecon. It stands on the crest of the mountain road connecting this town with Merthyr Tydfil and may be reached from either by bus. But it is now the South Glamorgan Youth Adventure Centre, and the nearest Youth Hostel is at Llwyn y Celyn, some two miles distant.

Trecastle has the nearest hotel to Carmarthen Fan and there is a Youth Hostel at Llanddeusant. The starting point of the ascent is 20 miles from Brecon which has ample accommodation.

Glossary of Welsh place-names

Readers who do not speak the Welsh language may have some difficulty in understanding the various place-names given to the different topographical features of the Principality. I hope, therefore, the translation of some of them as set out below will be useful to travellers and climbers in this delectable country.

Aber, a river mouth
Ach, water
Aderyn, a bird
Ael, a brow or edge
Afon, a river
Allt, a wooded slope
Aran, a high place
Arddu, a black crag

Bach, little
Bala, a lake outlet
Ban, peak, crest, beacon
Bedd, a grave
Ber, a hilltop.
Bera, *Bere*, beak, top, point
Betws, a chapel
Beudy, a byre or cowhouse
Blaen, the head of a valley
Boch, a cheek
Bod, a home or abode
Bont, a bridge
Braich, an arm or branch
Bran, a crow
Bras, thick or fat
Brith, speckled
Bron, the slope of a hill
Brwynog, marshy
Bryn, an eminence
Bwlch, a pass
Bychan, small

Cadair, a chair or throne
Cae, an enclosed field
Caer, a camp or fortress
Cafn, a trough
Canol, middle
Capel, a chapel
Carn, a cairn or heap of stones
Carnedd, a cairn
Carreg, stone
Caseg, a mare
Castell, a castle or fortress
Cau, a hollow
Cefn, a ridge
Celyn, holly
Cidwm, a wolf
Clogwyn, a cliff or precipice
Clwyd, a gate
Clyd, a shelter
Cnicht, a knight

Coch, red
Coed, a wood
Congl, a corner
Cors, a bog or swamp
Craig, a rock or crag
Crib, a ridge or jagged edge
Cribin, the small crest of a hill
Croes, a cross
Crug, a mound
Cwm, a hollow or coombe
Cwn, dogs
Cymer, a confluence

Dau, two
Dinas, a natural fortress
Dol, a dale or meadow
Drosgl, a rough hill
Drum, a ridge
Drws, a door
Du or *ddu*, black
Dwr, water
Dyffryn, a wide valley
Dysgl, a dish or plate

Eglwys, a church
Eigiau, a shoal of fish
Eira, snow
Erw, an acre
Eryi, a highland
Esgair, a shank or limb

Fach, small
Faes, a field or meadow
Fan, peak, crest, beacon
Fawr, large
Felin, a mill
Ffordd, a road
Ffynnon, a well or fountain
Foel, a bare or bald hill
Fyny, upwards

Gaer, a camp
Gafr, a goat
Gallt, a slope
Ganol, middle
Gardd, a garden
Garn, an eminence
Garth, an enclosure
Gawr, a torrent
Glas, blue-green
Gludair, a heap
Glyn, a deep valley
Goch, red
Golau, a light or beacon
Golwg, a view
Gors, a swamp
Grach, scabby
Groes, a cross
Grug, heather
Gwastad, a plain
Gwern, an alder coppice
Gwyn, white
Gwynt, wind

Hafod, a summer dwelling
Hebog, a hawk
Helgi, a hunting dog
Helyg, willows
Hen, old
Heulog, sunny
Hir, long
Hydd, a stag

Isaf, lower

Las, blue-green
Llan, a church
Llech, a flat stone
Llefn, smooth
Llithrig, slippery
Lloer, moon
Llwyd, grey
Llwyn, a grove
Llyn, a lake
Llys, a hall
Lon, a lane

Maen, a block of stone
Maes, a field or meadow
Man, a place
Mawr, large
Meirch, horses
Melin, a mill
Melyn, yellow
Mign, a bog
Min, lip or edge
Mir fair
Moch, pigs
Moel, a bare or bald hill
Mor, sea
Morfa, flat seashore—sea fen
Mur, a wall
Mynach, a monk
Mynydd, a mountain

Nant, a brook
Newydd, new

Oer, cold
Og, harrow
Ogof, a cave
Oleu, light
Onn, an ash tree

Pair, a cauldron
Pant, a hollow
Parc, an enclosure
Pen, a peak or top
Penrhyn, a promontory
Pentre, a village
Perfedd, centre
Perth, a hedgerow bush
Pistyll, the spout of a waterfall
Plas, a mansion
Poeth, hot
Pont, a bridge
Porth, a port, gateway
Pwll, a pool

Rhaeadr, a waterfall
Rhiw, hill or slope
Rhyd, a passage or ford
Rhyn, a cape

Saeth, an arrow
Sarn, a causeway
Silin, spawn
Sych, dry

Tal, end
Tan, under
Tir, soil
Tomen, a mound
Traeth, sandy shore
Tref, a town
Tri, three

Trum, a ridge
Twll, a cavern
Twr, a tower
Ty, a house
Tyddyn, a small farmstead

Uchaf, upper or higher
Un, one

Waun, moorland
Wen, white
Wern, an alder swamp
Wrach, a witch
Wrth, near

Y—Yr, the
Yn, in
Ynys, an island
Ysfa, a sheep walk
Ysgol, a ladder
Ysgubor, a barn
Ystrad, a street or dale
Ystum, a curve or bend
Ystwyth, winding

The Welsh Peaks

56 Routes of ascent

The Snowdon Group Map 1

1 Pen-y-pass and Crib Goch
2 The Pyg Track
3 The Miners' Track
4 Lliwedd and Bwlch y Saethau
5 The Watkin Path
6 Yr Aran and Bwlch Main
7 Rhyd-ddu and Llechog
8 The Snowdon Ranger
9 The Llanberis Path
10 Cwm Glas

The Glyders Group Map 2

GLYDER FAWR

11 Ogwen Cottage and the Devil's Kitchen
12 Cwm Idwal and the Nameless Cwm
13 The Gribin
14 Llyn Bochlwyd, Bristly Ridge and Glyder Fach
15 Ogwen Cottage and Tyfan Scree Gully
16 The North Ridge of Tryfan
17 Heather Terrace
18 Bwlch Caseg-fraith
19 Gallt yr Ogof
20 The Ridge from Capel Curig
21 Pen-y-gwryd and the Miners' Track
22 Pen-y-gwryd and Llyn Cwmffynnon
23 Pen-y-pass and Esgair Felen
24 Nant Peris and Llyn y Cwn
24a Nant Peris and Elidir Fawr

Y GARN AND FOEL GOCH

25 Ogwen Cottage and Llyn Clyd
26 Ogwen Cottage and the Devil's Kitchen

The Carneddau Maps 3 and 4
27 Llyn Crafnant and Clogwyn Mawr
28 Creigiau Gleision
29 Penllithrig-y-wrach
30 Pen yr Helgi-du
31 Helyg, Craig yr Ysfa and Carnedd Llwyelyn
32 Llyn Ogwen and Carnedd Ddafydd
33 Ogwen Cottage and Pen yr Ole Wen
34 Bethesda and Carnedd Llywelyn
35 Aber Falls and Carnedd Llywelyn

The Moel Siabod Group Maps 5 and 6
36 The Royal Bridge and Moel Siabod
37 Cyfyng Falls, Uyn y Foel and Moel Siabod
38 Cnicht by the Dog Lakes
39 Cnicht by Llyn Llagi
40 Cnicht from Croesor
41 The Moelwyns from Croesor

The Moel Hebog Group Map 7
42 Beddgelert and Moel Hebog
43 The Nantlle Ridge
44 Craig y Bere and Mynydd Mawr

Cadair Idris Map 8
45 Tal-y-llyn, Cwm y Cau and Pen y Gadair

The Harlech Dome Map 9
46 The Roman Steps and Rhinog Fawr
47 Nant Col and Rhinog Fach

The Arennigs Map 10
48 Bala, Llyn Arennig Fawr and Arennig Fawr

The Arans Map 11
49 Dinas Mawddwy and Drysgol

Plynlimon Map 12
50 Dyffryn Castell and Eisteddfa Gurig

The Black Mountains Map 13
51 The Gadair Ridge

The Brecon Beacons Map 14
52 Bailea and Pen y Fan

Carmarthen Fan
53 Gwyn Arms and Fan Hir
54 Bwlch y Giedd
55 Llaudeusant

Heights of the principal Welsh Peaks

Arranged in order of altitude, in feet O.D. with their mountain group

1	3,560	Yr Wyddfa	Snowdon
2	3,493	Crib y Ddysgl, Carnedd Ugain	Snowdon
3	3,484	Carnedd Llywelyn	Carneddau
4	3,426	Carnedd Ddafydd	Carneddau
5	3,279	Glyder Fawr	Glyders
6	3,262	Glyder Fach	Glyders
7	3,210	Pen yr Ole Wen	Carneddau
8	3,195	Foel Grach	Carneddau
9	3,152	Yr Elen	Carneddau
10	3,104	Y Garn	Glyders
11	3,091	Foel Fras	Carneddau
12	3,029	Elidir Fawr	Glyders
13	3,023	Crib Goch	Snowdon
14	3,010	Tryfan	Glyders
15	2,970	Aran Fawddwy	Arans
16	2,947	Y Lliwedd	Snowdon
17	2,927	Pen y Cadair	Cadair Idris
18	2,907	Pen y Fan	Brecon Beacons
19	2,901	Aran Benllyn	Arans
20	2,875	Yr Aryg	Carneddau
21	2,863	Corn Du	Brecon Beacons
22	2,860	Moel Siabod	Moel Siabod
23	2,804	Mynydd Moel	Cadair Idris
24	2,800	Arennig Fawr	Arennigs
25	2,749	Llwytmor	Carneddau
26	2,732	Pen yr Helgi-du	Carneddau
27	2,726	Foel Goch	Glyders
28	2,694	Carnedd y Filiast	Glyders
29	2,664	Mynydd Perfedd	Glyders
30	2,660	Waun Fach	Black Mountains
31	2,636	Nameless, E Llyn Caseg-fraith	Glyders

32	2,632	Bannau Brycheiniog	Carmarthen Fan
33	2,624	Pen y Gadair Fawr	Black Mountains
34	2,621	Penllithrig-y-wrach	Carneddau
35	2,608	Cribyn	Brecon Beacons
36	2,566	Moel Hebog	Moel Hebog
37	2,564	Elidir Fach	Glyders
38	2,557	Craig Cywarch	Arans
39	2,528	Drum	Carneddau
40	2,527	Moelwyn Mawr	Moel Siabod
41	2,499	Gallt yr Ogof	Glyders
42	2,475	Y Llethr	Harlech Dome
43	2,468	Pen Plynlimon Fawr	Plynlimon
44	2,464	Diffwys	Harlech Dome
45	2,451	Yr Aran	Snowdon
46	2,451	Moel Llyfnant	Arennigs
47	2,408	Craig Cwmsilyn	Nantlle Ridge
48	2,397	Drysgol	Arans
49	2,389	Craig Eigiau	Carneddau
50	2,382	Moel Eilio	Snowdon
51	2,362	Rhinog Fawr	Harlech Dome
52	2,360	Pen Allt Mawr	Black Mountains
53	2,334	Moelwyn Bach	Moel Siabod
54	2,333	Rhinog Fach	Harlech Dome
55	2,329	Trum y Ddysgl	Moel Hebog
56	2,301	Carnedd Goch	Moel Hebog
57	2,290	Mynydd Mawr	Moel Hebog
58	2,287	Allt Fawr	Moel Siabod
59	2,265	Cnicht	Moel Siabod
60	2,264	Arennig Fach	Arennigs
61	2,214	Creigiau Gleision	Carneddau
62	2,207	Moel Cynghorion	Snowdon
63	2,167	Tyrau Mawr	Cadair Idris
64	2,152	Moel Druman	Moel Siabod
65	2,148	Mynydd Talmignedd	Nantlle Ridge
66	2,124	Moel yr Hydd	Moel Siabod
67	2,094	Moel Lefn	Moel Hebog
68	2,080	Y Garn II	Nantlle Ridge

69	2,034	Pen y Castell	Carneddau
70	2,032	Gallt y Wenallt	Snowdon
71	2,020	Moel yr Ogof	Moel Hebog
72	2,019	Gurn Wigau	Carneddau
73	2,000	Tal y Fan	Carneddau

The principal Welsh lakes

This list includes the more important Lynnaedd viewed from the routes to the peaks. They are enumerated alphabetically under each mountain group, their height above O.D. is given in feet when known, together with their approximate situation.

Snowdon

Bwlch Cwm-llan	—	Col between Yr Aran and Bwlch Main
Coch	1,705	Cwm Clogwyn
Du'r Arddu	1,901	Cwm Brwynog
Ffynnon-y-gwas	1,381	Cwm Clogwyn
Glas	—	Cwm Glas
Glas	—	Cwm Clogwyn
Glaslyn	1,971	Cwm Dyli
Gwynant	217	Vale of Gwynant
Llydaw	1,416	Cwm Dyli
Nadroedd	—	Cwm Clogwyn
Teyrn	1,237	Cwm Dyli

Glyders

Bochlwyd	1,806	Between Tryfan and Y Gribin
Caseg-fraith	—	Above Cwm Tryfan
Cwm-y-ffynnon	1,254	N. of Pen-y-pass
Y Cwn	—	Immediately S. of Devil's Kitchen
Idwal	1,223	Above Ogwen Cottage
Padarn	840	N. of Llanberis
Peris	840	E. of Llanberis

Carneddau

Cowlyd	1,165	N. of Capel Curig
Crafnant	603	N.E. of Capel Curig
Dulyn	1,747	W. side of Cwm Eigiau

Eigiau	1,219	N. of Penllithrig-y-wrach
Ffynnon Lloer	—	N. of Llyn Ogwen
Ffynnon Llugwy	1,786	W. of Pen yr Helgi-du
Ffynnon Llyffaint	2,725	E. of Carnedd Llywelyn
Geirionydd	616	N. of Ugly House
Melynllyn	2,094	W. side of Cwm Eigiau
Ogwen	984	Crest of Nant Ffrancon
Moel Siabod		
Yr Adar	1,874	N.E. of Cnicht
Y Biswail	—	N. end of Cnicht ridge
Croesor	—	N. of Moelwyn Mawr
Cwmcorsiog	—	N. of Llyn Croesor
Dinas	176	Vale of Gwynant
Diwaunedd	1,208	Below W. ridge of Moel Siabod
Edno	1,797	N. of Cnicht
Y Foel	1,756	Immediately E. of Moel Siabod
Llagi	1,238	Immediately W. of Llyn yr Adar
Lockwood	890	Pen-y-gwryd
Mymbyr	588	Capel Curig
Moel Hebog		
Cwellyn	464	E. of Mynydd Mawr
Cwm Silyn	1,105	W. end of Nantlle Ridge
Y Dywarchen	770	N.W. of Rhyd-ddu
Y Gadair	598	S. of Rhyd-ddu
Nantlle Uchaf	322	W. end of Drws-y-coed Pass
Cadair Idris		
Y Cau	1,552	S. of Pen y Gader
Y Gadair	—	Immediately below Pen y Gader
Tal-y-llyn	270	S. of Dolgellau
Harlech Dome		
Arddyn	1,029	E. of Llawr Llech
Y Bi	—	S. of Rhinog Fach
Bodlyn	1,245	E. of Diffwys

Cwmbychan	605	Below the Roman Steps
Du	—	N. of Rhinog Fawr
Dulyn	—	S. of Y Llethr
Gloy	—	N. of Rhinog Fawr
Hywel	—	S. of Rhinog Fach
Morwynion	—	Bwlch Tyddiad
Perfeddau	—	N.W. of Y Llethr
The Arennigs		
Arrenig Fawr	1,326	S.E. of the old Arennig Station
The Arans		
Tegid Bala	530	N. of Aran Benllyn
Creiglyn Dyfi	—	Immediately E. of Aran Fawddwy
Plynlimon		
Llygad Rheidol	—	Due N. of summit
Black Mountains		
Grwyne Fawr	1,627	N.E. of Gadair Ridge
Brecon Beacons		
Cwm-llwch	—	N.W. of Corn Du
Carmarthen Fan		
Llyn y Fan Fawr		East of summit
Llyn y Fan Fach		West of summit

Mountain photography

I have already written and lectured extensively on this fascinating branch of photography, and in my *Snowdon Holiday* I included copious notes on its application to the mountains of North Wales. But since this work has been out of print for some years, it may be useful to deal more fully with the subject herein than I did in its companion volume, *The Lakeland Peaks*. Moreover, I receive innumerable requests for tips from climbers who collect my works, and the following information may incidentally relieve me of much voluminous correspondence.

1 **The ideal camera for the mountaineer** is undoubtedly the modern miniature owing to its compact form, quick manipulation, great depth of focus, variety of lenses and thirty-six frames on each spool of film. While these instruments are represented in their best and most expensive type by the Leica, Pentax and Nikon series, it does not follow that other less costly makes will not give good photographs. Recently I had the opportunity of making a comparative set of colour transparencies with the Leica and a camera that sold retail for about £12, and had I not been critical I should have been satisfied with the latter; for if you require a camera for your own pleasure and merely wish to show the prints or transparencies to your friends, then why pay over £100 for the instrument? In any case, I recommend that you consult your local dealer who will be happy to demonstrate the differences between the various makes and prices.

2 **The lens** is the most important feature, and the best of them naturally facilitate the perfect rendering of the subject. A wide aperture is not essential, because it is seldom necessary to work out of doors at anything greater than F/4.5. It is advisable to use the objective at infinity in mountain

photography because overall sharpness is then obtained, and to stop down where required to bring the foreground into focus. It is in this connection that the cheaper camera, which of course is fitted with an inexpensive lens, falls short of its more costly competitors; for the latter are corrected for every known fault and the resulting photographs are then not only more acceptable for enlarged reproduction but also yield exhibition prints of superlative quality. Three lenses are desirable in this branch of photography: 1. a 28mm or 35mm wide angle; 2. a standard 50mm which is usually supplied with most cameras; and 3. a 90mm long focus. These cover every likely requirement: the wide angle is most useful when *on* a mountain or lofty ridge; the 50mm encompasses the average scene, such as hill and valley; and the long focus is an advantage when the subject is very distant.

An analysis of their use in this region is as follows:

Wide angle	50 per cent
Standard	40 per cent
Long focus	10 per cent

3 *A lens hood* is an indispensable accessory, because it cuts out adventitious light and increases the brilliance and clarity of the picture. Many climbers have the illusion that this gadget is only required when the sun is shining and that it is used to keep the direct rays out of the lens when facing the light source. While its use is then imperative, they overlook the fact that light is reflected from many points of the hemisphere around the optical axis, and it is the interception of this incidental light that is important.

4 **A filter** is desirable, especially for the good rendering of skyscapes. A pale orange yields the most dramatic results, providing there are not vast areas of trees in the landscape in which all detail would be lost. It is safer to use a yellow filter, which does not suffer from this defect, and with autumn colours a green filter is very effective. *The exposure factors* do not differ materially, and in view of the wide latitude of

modern black-and-white film the resulting slight differences in density can be corrected when printing. *For colour work* a skylight filter, formerly known as Wratten 1a, is useful for reducing the intensity of the blues and for eliminating haze.

5 **Panchromatic film** is to be preferred for landscapes, and the speed of modern types has been increased substantially, so much so that those having a Weston or ASA meter rating of up to 125 will yield grainless negatives providing they are processed with the developer that is recommended by the makers.

6 **Exposure and development** are co-related. From May to September with bright sunlight and well-distributed clouds, films of the above speed require an average exposure of 1/250th of a second at an aperture of F/8 or 11 with a 2 × yellow filter, processed with a fine-grain developer for 8 minutes at a temperature of 68°F. Such negatives should be brilliantly clear and not too contrasty, and they will print on normal paper.

7 **The best time of year** for photography among the Welsh Peaks is the month of May. A limpid atmosphere and fine cumulus are then a common occurrence and less time is wasted in waiting for suitable lighting. Colour work at this time is also satisfactory because the landscape still reveals the reds of the dead bracken, which, however, disappear in June with the rapid growth of the new fresh green fronds. Nevertheless, the most dramatic colour transparencies are obtained during the last week in October because the newly dead bracken is then a fiery red, the grass has turned to golden yellow, and the long shadows increase the contrast between peak and valley.

8 **Lack of sharpness** is a problem that causes disappointment to some amateurs, and they are often apt to blame the lens

when the complaint is in fact due to camera shake. It is one thing to hold the instrument steady at ground level with a good stance and no strong wind to disturb the balance, while it is quite another problem in the boisterous breezes on the lofty ridges of Wales. When these conditions prevail, it is risky to use a lower speed than that indicated above, and maximum stability may be achieved by leaning against a slab of rock or in a terrific gale of wind by even lying down and jamming the elbows into the spaces between the crags; but foreground should never be sacrificed on this account. In calm weather a light tripod may be used, but in all other conditions it is too risky to erect one and have it blown over a precipice!

9 **Lighting** is the key to fine mountain photography, and the sun at an angle of 45 degrees, over the left or right shoulder, will yield the required contrasts. These conditions usually appertain in the early morning or the late evening. If possible avoid exposures at midday with the sun overhead when the lighting is flat and uninteresting. Before starting on any climb, study the topography of your mountain so that full advantage can be taken of the lighting. Moreover, never be persuaded to discard your camera when setting out in bad weather, because the atmosphere in the hills is subject to the most sudden and unexpected changes, and sometimes wet mornings develop into fine afternoons, with magnificent clouds and limpid lighting. If your camera is then away back in your lodgings, you may live to regret the omission.

10 **The Sky** is often the saving feature in mountain photographs since cloudless conditions or a sunless landscape seldom yield a pleasing picture. See plate 3.

11 **Haze** is one of the bugbears in this branch of photography, and these conditions are especially prevalent among the Welsh Peaks during July and August. If an opalescent effect is desired, this is the time of year to secure it,

Plate 3 Cloud over the Glyders and Tryfan, seen from Clogwyn Mawr

but while such camera studies may be favoured by the purist, they seldom appeal to the climber who prefers to see the detail he knows exists in his subjects.

12 **Colour Photography** has been simplified in recent years by the introduction of cameras in which both exposure and aperture can be automatically adjusted to light conditions, and in consequence failures are rare. Owing to the narrow latitude of colour film correct exposure is essential if the resulting transparency is to approximate in hue to that of the landscape as seen by the eye. The only certain way to achieve success in all weather conditions is to *use a meter before making each exposure* and to be sure it is pointed at the same angle as the camera. This is most important, because if more sky is included in the meter than in the lens a shorter exposure will be indicated and this will result in an under-exposed transparency in which the colour will be unduly intensified, whereas if the two operations are reversed it will be weakened. Excellent results are obtainable with Kodachrome 25 when an exposure of 1/250 second at an aperture of F/5.6 in sunlight between 10 a.m. and 4 p.m. during the summer months should produce satisfactory transparencies which may be viewed most advantageously by projection. However, *faster* colour film is now available up to ASA 100, when an exposure of about 1/250 second at an aperture of F/8 or 11 yields superlative transparencies.

13 **Design or composition** is the most outstanding feature of a good camera study; that is, one that not only immediately appeals to the eye, but rather one that can be lived with afterwards. Everything I have so far written herein on this subject comes within the scope of *technique*, and anyone who is prepared to give it adequate study and practice should be able to produce a good negative, and from it a satisfying print.

But to create a picture that far transcends even the best

snapshot requires more than this and might well be described as a flair, or if you like a seeing eye that immediately appreciates the artistic merits of a particular mountain scene. And strangely enough those who possess this rare gift usually produce a certain type of picture which is indelibly stamped with their personality; so much so that it is often possible to name the photographer as soon as his work is displayed. And, moreover, while this especial artistic trait may be developed after long application of the basic principles of composition, the fact remains that it is not the camera that really matters, for it is merely a tool, but the person behind the viewfinder, who, when satisfied with the design of his subject, ultimately and quite happily releases the shutter.

To the painter, composition is relatively easy, because he can make it conform to the basic principles of art by moving a tree to one side of his picture, or by completely removing a house from the foreground, or by inducing a stream to flow in another direction, or by accentuating the real subject, if it happens to be a mountain, by moving it or by increasing or decreasing its angles to suit his tastes. A photographer on the other hand has to move himself and his camera here and there in order to get these objects in the right position in his viewfinder. When he moves to one side to improve the position of one of them, another is thrown out of place, or perhaps the lighting is altered. In many cases, therefore, a compromise is the only solution, because if he spends too much time in solving his problem the mood may change, when his opportunity would be lost. It is just this element in mountain photography that brings it into line with sport, and, like golf, it can be both interesting and exasperating. Of course, the critic can sit in a comfortable chair by a warm fire at home and pull a photograph to pieces. He does not, perhaps, realise that the person taking the picture may have been wandering about knee-deep in a slimy bog, or that a bitterly cold wind was sweeping across a lofty ridge and making his teeth chatter, or that the light was failing, or that he had crawled out on a rocky spur with a hundred-foot drop on either side to get his subject properly composed.

Assuming, therefore, both lighting and cloudscape are favourable, what are the essential features of good composition? In the first place, you must select a pleasing object that is accented by tonal contrast as the centre of interest; in the second, you must place this object in the most attractive position in the frame or picture space; and in the third, you must choose a strong and appropriate foreground. Or, in other words, when the weather is favourable the success or failure of your photograph will depend entirely upon the *viewpoint*.

Thus, if your subject happens to be Snowdon, I may be able to help you with a few hints about five of the illustrations in this book. It is generally agreed that the eastern aspect of this mountain is the finest and it looks its best up to noon on a sunny morning with cloud drifting overhead. But you must first decide whether you wish to make a picture of the majestic peak itself, or of the whole range; if the former, there is one matchless viewpoint, whereas if the latter, there are at least three and each one of them has a different type of foreground.

Let us begin with the peak itself, whose tonal contrast will be enhanced by side lighting; whose strongest placing in a vertical frame will be in the centre of the picture space, as seen on the jacket of this book, and in a horizontal frame in the upper right-hand third as in plate 4; and whose most appropriate foreground will be Llyn Llydaw. Now, you must remember that it is always the foreground that leads the eye into a picture, and the treatment of the lake is therefore of the utmost importance. In the first place, the distant shore must never form a horizontal line above the lower third; for if you place it in the centre it will cut the picture into two halves. Moreover, some bold rocks on the near shore will add strength and interest to the whole study, and if you have a friend with you, ask him to stand near the shore to impart scale to the picture.

The beauty of the graceful lines of the Snowdon group always delights the eye and one of the nearest viewpoints that

Plate 4 Snowdon from Llyn Llydaw

Plate 5 The Snowdon Group from Garth Bridge

Plate 6 Snowdon from the Royal Bridge, Capel Curig

Plate 7 Snowdon from the Pinnacles of Capel Curig

reveal them to advantage is Garth Bridge, above the little waterfall that enters the western end of Llynnau Mymbyr. The turbulent stream above the bridge, dappled with rocks and embellished by a single tree on the right, makes an excellent foreground for this photograph, as shown in plate 5. If you retreat farther from the range you will find another charming foreground in the Royal Bridge at the foot of Llynnau Mymbyr, but since Snowdon is now some ten miles distant its imposing character will be diminished if you do not use a long-focus lens. This allows the group to completely fill the frame and in your picture it will assume a similar magnitude to that seen by the eye, as seen in plate 6. A higher viewpoint has certain advantages and you will find one by walking up to the Pinnacles of Capel Curig. From the lowest of them you will secure a splendid photograph in which the twin lakes and Plas-y-Brenin yield a satisfactory foreground which leads the eye in one vast sweep to this magnificent mountain range, as shown in plate 7. Finally, whenever you take a shot of any of the Welsh Peaks, remember that it will be improved not only by placing a lake, a stream, a bridge, a figure or a group of climbers in the foreground, but also on occasion by introducing a tree or cottage or some object whose size if known will impart both interest and scale to your picture.

In conclusion, I would call your attention to the dramatic possibilities of photographing sunsets in colour; for by placing a still or slightly rippling lake in the foreground you will immensely enhance the whole picture by capturing the colour reflected by water as well as that already appearing in the sky.

Photography in the different groups

I have often been asked "What is the best view *of* such and such a mountain?" or "What is the most striking view *from* so and so?" These are difficult questions, because the answers depend so much upon one's personal tastes, which are influenced in no small degree by atmospheric conditions on any particular occasion. The present volume seems to be a convenient medium for an attempt to offer some guidance on this very debatable question, and while there are doubtless many who will disagree with my opinions, I shall give them for what they are worth. Where possible I have appended references to appropriate examples already portrayed in one or other of my works, as follows:

SL: *Snowdonia through the Lens*
SH: *Snowdon Holiday*
WW: *Wanderings in Wales*
EH: *Escape to the Hills*
WP: *The Welsh Peaks* (the present work)

The number indicates the plate in the particular volume, to which I have added the most suitable time of day for photographing the subject (G.M.T.). It should be noted that the examples given were not necessarily taken at the best time or season.

The suggestions are arranged according to the grouping system adopted throughout this work and under two headings: (1) the best pictorial views *of* the groups or their separate tops; (2) The most striking views *from* the groups. After what I have already written herein it will be obvious that foreground interest is of paramount importance since it bears a direct relationship to the pictorial rendering of the main subject.

The best pictorial views of the group

The eastern aspect of Snowdon

(*a*) From Llyn Llydaw before noon. SL 1; SH 52; EH 203; WP 4 & 18.
(*b*) From Crib Goch before noon. SH 57; EH 208; WP 12.
(*c*) From Garth Bridge before noon. WP 5.
(*d*) From Llynnau Mymbyr any time of day. LS jacket; EH 1; EH 176.
(*e*) From the Royal Bridge before noon. SL 5; EH 169; WP 6.
(*f*) From the Pinnacles of Capel Curig before noon. WP7.

The western aspect of Snowdon

(*a*) From Y Garn II after 2 p.m. SH 43; WP 184 & 187.
(*b*) From Craig y Bere and Mynydd Mawr after 2 p.m. WP 202

The northern aspect of Snowdon

(*a*) From the Glyders before noon. SL 34; WP 79.
(*b*) From Llyn Padarn after 4 p.m. WP 55.
(*c*) From Y Garn after 4 p.m. WP 109.

Crib Goch

(*a*) From Pen-y-pass before 11 a.m. SL 51; EH 207.
(*b*) From Crib y Ddysgl after 2 p.m. SL 53; WP 13.
(*c*) From Cwm Glas after 3 p.m. SH 1; WP 62.

Lliwedd

(*a*) From Llyn Llydaw before 10 a.m. SH 66.
(*b*) From the Snowdon Horseshoe after 4 p.m. SH 68; EH 213; WP 11.

Yr Aran

From Llyn Gwynant before 11 a.m. SL 42; WW 202; WP 33.

The Glyders

From upper Nant Ffrancon after 4 p.m.

Tryfan

(*a*) From Helyg before 11 a.m. SL 14; SH 76; Sunset SL 61; WP 85.
(*b*) From Caseg-fraith Ridge before 11 a.m. SL 27; WP 1 & 86.

Bristly Ridge

From Llyn Caseg-fraith before 11 a.m. SL 28; WW 188; EH 192; WP 89.

Cwm Idwal

From Pen yr Ole Wen after 5 p.m. summer. SL 23; WP 147.

Y Garn

From head of Llyn Ogwen before 11 a.m. WP 106.

Carneddau

(*a*) From the Pinnacles of Capel Curig before noon. SL 12.
(*b*) Craig yr Ysfa from Cwm Eigiau before 11 a.m. SH 7; WP 134.
(*c*) Black Ladders from Carnedd Ddafydd after 4 p.m. WP 143.

Moel Siabod

(*a*) From near the Ugly House before noon. SL 10.
(*b*) From the path to Llyn Crafnant before 11 a.m.
(*c*) From Clogwyn Mawr after 4 p.m.

Cnicht

From Tan Lan after 3 p.m. EH 187; SH 35; WP 160.

The Moelwyns

From the Afon Glaslyn after 3 p.m. WW 178; WP 174.

Moel Hebog

(*a*) From Llyn Dinas before noon. SL 44.
(*b*) From the Afon Glaslyn before noon. EH 198.
(*c*) From Pont Cae'r-gors after 5 p.m. SH 33.

(*d*) Y Garn II and Craig y Bere from Llyn y Gadair before 11 a.m. WP 185.
(*e*) Craig y Bere from Llyn y Dywarchen before noon. WP 199.
(*f*) Mynydd Mawr from the Snowdon Ranger before 11 a.m. WP 48.
(*g*) Mynydd Mawr from Waun-fawr after 3 p.m. WP 204.

Cadair Idris
(*a*) From the north after 5 p.m. summer, WW 104; WP 205.
(*b*) Craig y Cau from the east before 11 a.m. WW 106; WP 207.
(*c*) Pen y Gader from Cyfrwy after 3 p.m. WW 109; WP 211.

The Harlech Dome
(*a*) From the east before 11 a.m. WW 154; WP 213.
(*b*) Rhinog Fach from Llyn Hywel after noon. WW 161; WP 216.

The Arennigs
From the north-west after 4 p.m. WW 148.

The Arans
(*a*) From Bala Lake after 5 p.m. WW 135.
(*b*) Aran Benllyn from Drysgol before noon. WW 125; WP 223.

Plynlimon
(*a*) From the south any time of day. WP 227.
(*b*) From Eisteddfa Gurig before noon. WW 91; WP 230.

The Black Mountains
From Skirrid Fawr before 11 a.m. WW 24; WP 231.

The Brecon Beacons
(*a*) From the Golf Course at Cradoc in late afternoon. WP 235.

(*b*) Pen y Fan from Cribyn before noon. QW 24; WP 237.

Carmarthen Fan

(*a*) Eastern escarpment from Standard Stone in the morning. WP 236.

(*b*) North Western Cwms from Spot Height 458 in the afternoon.

The most striking views from the groups

Snowdon

(*a*) The Glyders and Crib Goch up to 3 p.m. SL 54; WP 14.

(*b*) Lliwedd and Llyn Llydaw after 4 p.m. SH 65; WP 15.

Crib Goch

(*a*) The Horseshoe before noon. SH 57; WP 12.

(*b*) The Ridge and Pen y Pass up to 3 p.m. SH 61.

(*c*) Llyn Glas and the Llnaberis Lakes up to noon. SH 62.

Clogwyn station

Llanberis Pass any time of day. WP 57.

Yr Aran

(*a*) The South Ridge of Snowdon up to 2 p.m. WW 201; WP 34.

(*b*) Moel Siabod and Llyn Gwynant about noon. WW 203; WP 37.

(*c*) Mynydd Mawr and Llyn Cwellyn before noon. WW 204; WP 36.

The Glyders

(*a*) Tryfan from Llyn Caseg-fraith before noon. WP 88.

(*b*) Snowdon and the Castle of the Winds before 11 a.m. SL 43; WP 79.

(*c*) The Devil's Kitchen from above after 4 p.m. SL 39; WP 102.

(*d*) Cwm Glas from Esgair Felen after 4 p.m. SH 46; WP 98.
(*e*) The Glyders from Y Garn after 2 p.m. WP 110.

Carneddau

(*a*) Sunset from Carnedd Llywelyn, 5 p.m. onwards. SL 26; WP 138.
(*b*) Snowdon and Cwm Idwal from Pen yr Ole Wen after 5 p.m. summer. WP 147.
(*c*) Tryfan and Llyn Ogwen from Pen yr Ole Wen after 3 p.m. SL 24; WP 146.
(*d*) Ogwen Valley from Clogwyn Mawr before noon. WP 117.
(*e*) Llyn Crafnant from Clogwyn Mawr all day. SL 4; WP 116.

Moel Siabod

(*a*) Western panorama comprising Hebog and Snowdon before noon. WP 156.
(*b*) Cwm Dyli from Clogwyn Bwlch-y-maen in the morning.
(*c*) Snowdon Horseshoe from Llyn Edno up to 2 p.m. SH 21; WP 162.
(*d*) Snowdonia panorama from Cnicht any time of day. WP 164, 165 & 166.

Moel Hebog

(*a*) Beddgelert and the Vale of Gwynant up to 3 p.m. SH 32; EH 197; WP 182.
(*b*) Snowdon from Y Garn II after 2 p.m. SH 43; WP 184 & 187.
(*c*) Snowdon from Craig y Bere after noon. WP 202.
(*d*) Nantlle Ridge from Craig Cwmsilin any time of day. WP 194.

Cadair Idris

(*a*) Snowdon and the Harlech Dome from Cyfwry all day. WW 110; WP 209.
(*b*) Mawddach Estuary from Cyfrwy all day. WW 111; WP 210

The Harlech Dome

(*a*) The Ridge from Rhinog Fawr after 2 p.m. WW 159; WP WP 214.

(*b*) Y Llethr from above Llyn Hywel after 2 p.m. WW 163; WP 218.

The Arennigs

Panorama of Snowdonia and Mid-Wales all day.

The Arans

Cadair Idris from Aran Fawddwy before noon.

The Brecon Beacons

(*a*) Corn Du from Pen y Fan in the morning. WW 36; WP 238.

(*b*) Llyn Cwm-llwch from Corn Du in the morning. WW 37; WP 239.

Carmarthen Fan

(*a*) The Brecon Beacons in the afternoon. WP 246.

Notes on the Routes

I have divided the Welsh Peaks into *twelve Mountain Groups* for the sake of convenience and easy reference. They commence with Snowdon because it is the highest mountain in the Principality and its ascent the most esteemed. The groups in this particular part of the region follow each other in clockwise sequence and end with the Moel Hebog range. *The Routes* to the dominating peak in each group are also arranged clockwise wherever possible so that they fit into the general scheme and thus avoid undue cross reference. This arrangement facilitates the choice of those routes which are more or less adjacent, as for instance the Rhyd-ddu Path and the Snowdon Ranger, where one of them can be ascended and the other descended. But I have purposely omitted any description of the *Descents* because when the ascents are reversed they obviously answer this requirement, *The Panorama* from the reigning peak in each group is always described at the termination of its first ascent. Many of the routes involve the traverse of subsidiary tops and the conspicuous features revealed from them are noted in passing, despite the fact that there may be a similarity in the views when the peaks are near together.

Farther south, however, I have not been able to follow this scheme because the ranges are more scattered. I have therefore first given details of Cadair Idris since it is the most popular peak and terminated the descriptions with that of Carmarthen Fan, which is one of the least known mountains in Wales.

Many of these attractive ranges have been sadly neglected by climbers, perhaps because they are less spectacular than those in North Wales. I have therefore described and illustrated only the route which discloses the finest topography in each group, but in many of them the terrain is relatively easy and other ways of reaching the summits may be worked out on the spot with little risk.

Distances and times

These questions always involve a certain amount of speculation in mountaineering and I have purposely omitted any detailed reference to them in this work. *The Distances* may be calculated approximately from the maps, which are one inch to the mile, but it should be remembered that a map mile may in fact be considerably more than that owing to the undulating nature of the ground. *The Times* depend not only upon the pace and rhythm of each climber, but also upon the topography of the mountain as well as weather conditions. The best way to calculate them is to use the formula of Naismith, which allows one hour for each three map miles, plus half an hour for every 1,000 feet of ascent. This is fairly accurate for ordinary hill walking under favourable conditions, and while it includes reasonable halts for food and for viewing the grandeur of the mountain scene, it does not allow for bad weather, snow, rock climbing or photography, since the latter often involves much delay in finding the most effective foreground for any particular picture and for awaiting favourable lighting.

To make the application of this system clear, I will illustrate it by calculating the distance and time required for the complete circuit of the Snowdon Horseshoe, which is described and portrayed in my *Snowdon Holiday*, but may also be checked by combining Routes 1 and 4 noted in this volume.

It is three map miles from Pen y Pass to the summit of Snowdon by way of Crib Goch, and four miles back over Lliwedd and past Llyn Llydaw. This makes a total of seven map miles, which according to the above formula will take about two and a half hours. Since the starting point is at a height of 1,169 feet, this must be subtracted from the altitude of the first top, Crib Goch, 3,023 – 1,169 = 1,854 feet. Below this top lies Bwlch Coch on the 2,816-foot contour, and thence to Carnedd Ugain at 3,493 feet adds 677 feet to the ascent. Then again the point of emergence on the skyline of the zigzags is 3,258 feet, which makes a further addition of 302 feet to reach the summit of Snowdon at 3,560 feet—a total height climbed of 2,833 feet. But this is not the last rise in the Horseshoe; for after descending to Bwlch y Saethau at 2,691 feet, there is a further ascent of 256 feet to the cairn on Lliwedd at 2,947 feet. This makes a grand total of 3,089 feet, which according to the above formula adds one and a half hours, thus allowing altogether four hours for the complete traverse in favourable weather. However, as no account has been taken of halts for viewing the scenery from the four tops, or for food, and even if no time is spent in photography about one hour should be added, making five hours a reasonable time for fit and strong pedestrians to complete the whole circuit.

Since this book will be read by men and women of all ages, these figures may be discouraging to those in advancing years, and in these circumstances I think it will be useful, and perhaps indeed inspiring, to give the times taken on my last walk over this magnificent lofty ridge. On May 8th, 1956, I was in my sixty-fifth year and at 10 a.m. a young friend and I left Pen y Pass after a previous day of heavy rain. It was a cold, sunny, invigorating morning and we never hurried anywhere but reached Bwlch y Moch in an hour and Crib Goch at noon. We left the cairn half an hour later and stood on the summit of Snowdon at 2 p.m. where we spent a lazy hour in resting and refreshment. We passed the stony top of Lliwedd at 4 p.m. and were back at our starting point at 6 p.m., thus taking eight leisurely hours for this wonderful walk. I already possessed a good collection of photographs of the Horseshoe, but on this occasion took a further twenty-four shots in monochrome and a similar number in colour, all of which involved time spent in discovering unusual viewpoints. So, to those of you in the sixties and seventies, I say, Have a Go!

Route finding in mist

In these not uncommon conditions it is imperative to know with certainty your exact location on the map when the mist comes down to engulf you in gloom and to immediately note the direction to be taken. If you are on a well-cairned track no difficulties should be encountered, but when this is not the case you must estimate the distance to the next known point and set a course accurately by using your companion as a sighting mark. Keep him in view ahead while frequently referring to the compass and use your aneroid to check the rise and fall in the ground. If you are familiar with the gradient this will help to control your direction, but take nothing for granted; always trust the compass excepting when among magnetic rocks, basaltic and gabbro formations such as exist in the Coolins of Skye, and pay no attention whatsoever to gratuitous advice as to direction from compassless companions. Avoid contouring a slope; if you do this, you will no longer be master of your direction. It is always advisable to go straight down and never to diverge from a supposed obstacle without actual trial, because mist exaggerates both size and distance.

Should you be in the unhappy position of having no compass but *are familiar with the terrain* work your way down slowly over grass but never enter a ravine or gully or endeavour to descend a series of steep crags, whereas if you are on a ridge keep to its declining crest and if it forks make sure you take the known branch. If, on the other hand, you are alone on an uncairned track and also unfamiliar with the ground, stay put until the mist clears sufficiently for you to find your way. In these conditions you are in a very dangerous situation because mist sometimes persists for days in mountainous country. It is much better to practise map and compass reading in clear weather so that in mist you will have a reasonable chance of finding your way to safety.

Accident procedure

Distress signal. *Six* long flashes or *six* long blasts of a whistle in quick succession followed by a pause of one minute. This is repeated again and again until assistance is forthcoming.

The reply to this signal is in a similar vein; that is *three* flashes or blasts of a whistle followed by a pause of one minute, repeated again and again.

Brocken spectres

These remarkable phenomena are confined to hill country, and in consequence may, with luck, be observed by any climber on the Welsh Peaks, especially if he happens to be on a ridge enclosing a cwm filled with mist. They appear as gigantic shadows seen on the surface of the mist and were first observed on the Brocken in Germany, hence the name, but are said to be an optical illusion because the shadow is quite close and of actual size. It is usually only possible for each climber to see his own spectre.

Glories

These appear as a coloured ring round the shadow cast by the climber on the mist in similar circumstances. Each member of a climbing party can see only his own glory.

Snow warning

Snowdonia is notorious for its winter accidents, often due to inexperienced walkers with neither ice axe nor crampons, who climb carelessly in the snow. For, while a well known route in summer may be clear and free from risk, the same one in winter can be transformed into a very dangerous snow trap.

Aside from the difficulties that may be encountered in heavy snow, conditions that create the most dangerous spots are due to the snow surface melting in the rising temperature and then freezing solid when the temperature drops in the night. A further snowfall will cover this deceptive area and anyone who treads it *on a slope* will fall, slide downhill out of control, and if there is a precipice below he will go over the edge and possibly lose his life.

The Snowdon group

Yr Wyddfa	3,560 feet	1,085 metres
Crib y Ddysgl	3,493 feet	1,065 metres
Bwlch Glas (zigzags)	3,258 feet	993 metres
Crib Goch	3,023 feet	921 metres
Y Lliwedd	2,947 feet	898 metres
Bwlch Coch	2,816 feet	858 metres
Bwlch y Saethau	2,691 feet	820 metres
Yr Aran	2,451 feet	747 metres
Moel Eilio	2,382 feet	726 metres
Moel Cynghorion	2,207 feet	673 metres
Gallt y Wenallt	2,032 feet	619 metres
Bwlch y Moch	1,925 feet	586 metres
Bwlch Cwmbrwynog	1,625 feet	495 metres

It is only right and proper that Snowdon should assume pride of place in the following pages, not so much because it is the dominating peak of Wales, but more especially as its elevation is perhaps the finest in the Principality and most of the routes to its summit admit of little variation. All of them are clearly defined throughout and five traverse lofty ridges for part of the way.

It is scarcely surprising that the most popular starting point is Pen y Pass, since Routes 1 and 4 together form the famous Horseshoe, a ridge "walk" that is full of interest all the way and reveals the mountain at its best. The fact that Pen y Pass stands on the 1,169-foot contour may mislead some climbers into supposing that the actual ascent is therefore reduced to less than 2,400 feet, but as I have shown in the monograph on *Distances and Times* this is really 2,833 feet owing to the undulations of the ridge. In view of this fact there is not much difference in the height to be climbed from some of the other starting points, such as Llyn Cwellyn, which involves about

Map 1
The Snowdon Group

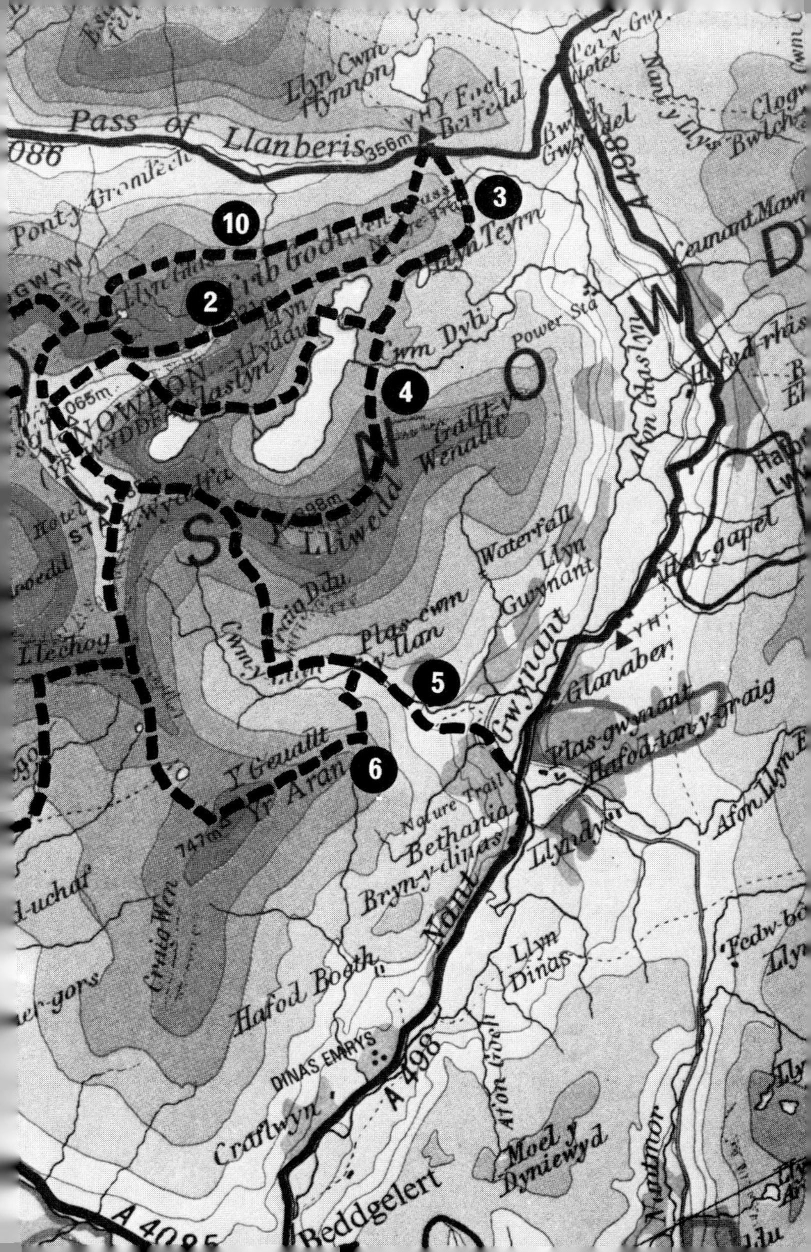

Pass of Llanberis
Llyn Cwm Ffynnon
356m
10
3
2
4
5
6
Crib Goch
Llyn Teyrn
Cwm Dyli
Power Sta
Llyn Llydaw
Glaslyn
1065m
SNOWDON
YR WYDDFA
Gallt-y-Wenallt
898m
Y Lliwedd
Waterfall
Llyn Gwynant
Plas-cwm-llan
Craig Ddu
Llechog
Y Geuallt
Yr Aran
747m
Nature Trail
Bethania
Bryn-y-dinas
Nant Gwynant
Glanaber
Plas-gwynant
Hafod-tan-y-graig
Llyndy
Afon Glaslyn
Ceunant Mawr
A498
Hafod Booth
Craig Wen
Llyn Dinas
DINAS EMRYS
Craflwyn
Moel y Dyniewyd
Beddgelert
Nantmor
A4085

Plate 8 Pen y Pass. Starting point of **Routes 1, 2, 3, 4 and 10**

3,000 feet, and Llanberis, 3,200 feet. The lowest point of departure is the Vale of Gwynant at about 200 feet and as the Watkin Path rises continuously it involves over 3,300 feet of ascent. But against these differences in altitude must be placed the length of the walk which from Pen y Pass is about three map miles, from Llyn Cwellyn and the Vale of Gwynant a little more and from Llanberis about five map miles. Then again the gradient has to be considered, and while the Llanberis Path is usually regarded as the easiest, those of the Snowdon Ranger and Watkin Path are a little harder, and that from Pen y Pass by way of Crib Goch is the steepest of them all.

All the routes described and illustrated herein are so well trodden that even in misty weather they should present no great difficulties, whereas in snow and mist they should be left severely alone, and especially so if snow lies on ice as this treacherous condition is often the cause of accidents in the most unsuspected places.

Snowdon

Route 1. Pen y Pass and Crib Goch. Leave the car park below the crest of the Llanberis Pass and follow the higher track which starts under the electricity pole, as waymarked; it rises along the northern flanks of the Last Nail in the Horseshoe right up to Bwlch y Moch. For most of the way the route mounts over boulders and scree and those climbers wearing Vibrams should be careful here as they are usually very slippery after rain. The path meanders over very rough ground and after passing through a collection of gigantic boulders it swings round to a derelict sheepfold at the base of some crags. This is the junction for the rather indistinct path over to the right which eventually leads into Cwm Glas. Ahead rises the broad, stony track to Bwlch y Moch, with Crib Goch towering overhead all the way. On attaining the pass the route forks; the left branch is the Pyg Track and the right branch our route to Crib Goch. At this point there is a fine view into Cwm Dyli, with Lliwedd on its far side and

Llyn Llydaw below. Our well-trodden path now steepens and while gaining height winds in and out of several rocky outcrops until, with the disappearance of grass, it begins to rise sharply. Ahead there is one tricky bit that is almost vertical, but a reliable hand-hold, high up on the right gives sufficient pull to pass this hazard safely. Beyond it nail marks lead upwards to the rocky staircase which eventually emerges by the cairn on our first summit.

The spacious prospect from Crib Goch is electrifying in its magnificence; for ahead the narrow rock ridge undulates as far as the Pinnacles which are crowned by the noble cone of Yr Wyddfa. To the L of the reigning peak the ridge falls to Bwlch y Saethau and then rises again to Lliwedd whose cliffs descend steeply to Llyn Llydaw far below. To the R, and beyond the Pinnacles, the ridge rises in steps from Bwlch Coch to Crib y Ddysgl, with the zigzags on its L and the Parson's Nose below on its R. Farther to the R there is a bird's-eye view into Cwm Glas, with its tiny lake cupped in the base of the hollow, and beyond it a distant view of the Llanberis Lakes. Still farther to the R rise the chain of the Glyders, separated from this lofty perch by the deep Llanberis Pass, whose road may be perceived as a thin white line far below.

Some 400 yards of knife-edge leads to the Pinnacles, but those with a steady head will experience no difficulties in crossing it in calm weather. These obstacles may be traversed by means of ample hand- and foot-holds, but those who prefer to avoid them may pass to the left and regain the track lower down. Bwlch Coch is soon encountered, with views on the L of Glaslyn at the foot of Yr Wyddfa, whence the track rises along the crest of the ridge, ascends an easy chimney on the R, and emerges immediately below Crib y Ddysgl. There are several paths on this broad shoulder, but do not take the one on the right because it leads to the top of the Parson's Nose, a cliff only suitable for experienced rock climbers. Beyond the summit of Carnedd Ugain the track descends gently and swings round to the left to Bwlch Glas, at the exit of the zigzags, and here the railway is encountered and

Plate 9 **Routes 1, 2, and 10**

Plate 10 **Routes 1 and 2**

Plate 11 The view from Bwlch y Moch on **Routes 1 and 2**

followed to the summit of Snowdon.

On a clear day the immense panorama unfolded from the large cairn on Snowdon is one of the finest in Britain, and despite the fact that it is possible to pick out the coast of Eire, the Isle of Man and Scafell Pike, in Lakeland, these objects are too far away to hold the gaze of the climber, and unconsciously his eye is drawn to the more attractive and closer detail of the landscape in the shape of the spurs of Snowdon itself. Of these, it is perhaps the sheer cliffs of Lliwedd that first attract his eye, but since the sun is always on the wrong side of this peak for its full appraisal, it is only natural to turn to the ridge he has just traversed enclosing the blue-green waters of Glasyln far below. It may well be that Crib Goch will rivet his attention by reason of its diminutive appearance, as it looks a long way below although there is a difference in altitude of barely 600 feet. Beyond the ridge rising to Crib y Ddysgl the solitudes of the Glyders appear tremendous and beyond them again there is a glimpse of Carnedd Llywelyn and Pen yr Ole Wen. To the east the twin Capel Lakes catch the light at the foot of Moel Siabod, and on swinging round to the south the cliffs of Cadair Idris stand out on the far horizon. Nearer at hand and in the south-west Moel Hebog is prominent, and the ridges of this group trail away to the north to end with the bold and compact form of Mynydd Mawr. The circle is completed with the glint of light on Llyn Cwellyn, R of which Moel Eilio leads the eye to the flat expanse of Anglesey and the sea.

It is always inspiring to stand on the highest peak south of the border and to scan the vast scenes described above, with the ground falling away at one's feet, but I never experience the same thrill here as I do on Crib Goch. On the latter I have the impression of complete detachment, coupled with the prospect of a higher peak ahead which has still to be conquered—and I look up. Here, however, on Yr Wyddfa, the peak has been won, the pendant ridges fall away—and I look down. Moreover, there is the constant reminder of other human beings, augmented during the summer season by the

Plate 12 **Route 1** The Snowdon Horseshoe from Crib Goch

Plate 13 **Route 1** The Paths on Crib y Ddysgl

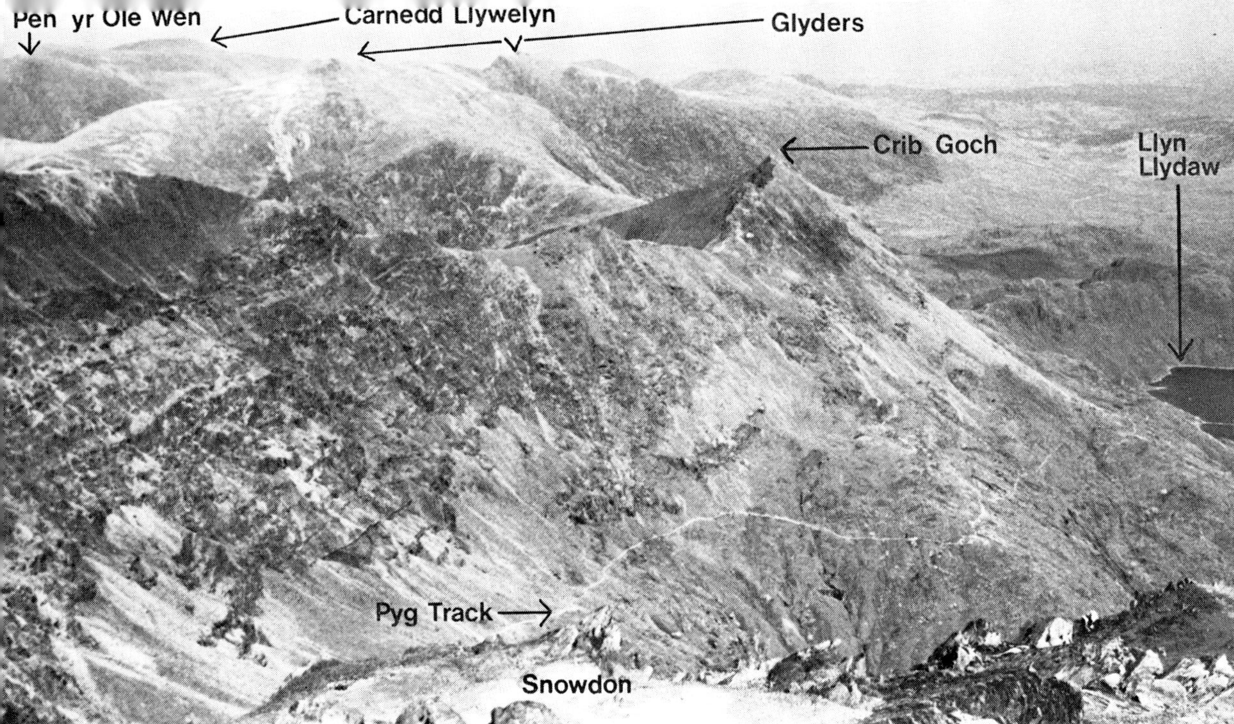

Plate 14 **Route 1** North-east from Snowdon

Plate 15 **Route 1** South-east from Snowdon

crowds that have not come up the hard way, and if you feel as I do, dear reader, walk over the Snowdon Horseshoe on a sunny day in early spring or late autumn when the profound solitude of this lofty ridge will act as balm to your soul.

Route 2. The Pyg Track. Follow Route 1 as far as Bwlch y Moch where the path forks and take the left branch which undulates slightly across the southern flanks of Crib Goch. It is well cairned throughout and one of the most popular routes to Snowdon, and, moreover, it has the advantage of disclosing on the L one of the most dynamic views of the majestic cliffs of Lliwedd beyond Llyn Llydaw. Yr Wyddfa towers into the sky ahead until a prominent cairn is reached above Glaslyn and it reveals this blue lake below at the foot of its precipices. At this point the track goes to the R and is soon joined by the Miners' Track coming up from this lake, whence the rough and steep ascent of the zig-zags lead to the skyline at Bwlch Glas, where Route 1 is joined and followed to the summit of the reigning peak.

Climbers who have recently ascended this Route will have noticed that erosion on a vast scale has occurred on the Zig-Zags, and indications of the amended route should be followed meticulously to minimise further trouble. A seven foot free standing monolith now marks the point of emergence of this track on Bwlch Glas, and in descent will be a most useful indication of the exact point at which to leave the ridge, invaluable in snow, mist and bad weather.

Route 3. The Miners' Track. Leave the car park at Pen y Pass by the old road leading to the Copper Mines. It is rough and stony, but rises at a gentle gradient with views on L of Moel Siabod and the sylvan Vale of Gwynant. It contours round the south-eastern slopes of the Last Nail in the Horseshoe, and at a sharp turn to R reveals Lliwedd, Snowdon and Crib Goch towering ahead. The route now takes a direct line for the peaks and passes round and above Llyn Teyrn on L, whose shore is marred by derelict buildings, and thereafter bears R

Plate 16 **Route 2**

Plate 17 **Routes 2 and 3** ascend the Zig-Zags

Plate 18 **Route 3**—Snowdon from Llyn Llydaw

Plate 19 **Route 3**

Plate 20 **Route 3**

Plate 21 **Route 3**

until Llyn Llydaw is reached. This is a superb viewpoint because it unveils one of the classic and most majestic prospects of Yr Wyddfa, while on L of it there is also a good view of Lliwedd. Keeping the lake on L, the broad track crosses its lower end by a causeway, which may be under water when the lake is full and then necessitates a detour to the R. The path winds along the shore of Llyn Llydaw, passes some unsightly and derelict mine buildings, and then turns sharp R when the first considerable rise is encountered. The path mounts on R of the stream coming down from Glaslyn, with Yr Wyddfa towering into the sky ahead, and later reaches the outflow of this sombre lake. Thence the level path rims its north shore, passes mine workings which should be avoided and more derelict buildings, until an eroded steep scree track on R rises to join the Pyg Track, when Route 2 is followed to the summit of Snowdon.

Route 4. Lliwedd and Bwlch y Saethau. Follow Route 3 to Llyn Llydaw and bear L on reaching the lake. The track rises gently at first, but do not take the rather indistinct branch on the R at the fork because this is used by rock climbers making for the cliffs of Lliwedd. Thence the path deteriorates and becomes very rough as it rises steeply to the col between Gallt y Wenallt on the L and Lliwedd Bach on the R. There is a prominent cairn on the ridge that is a useful landmark in mist. Now turn R and keep to the crest of the ridge, with sensational drops on the R, first over the lesser eminence of Lliwedd Bach and thereafter over the East Peak of Lliwedd, where the precipices on the R disappear into space, with Llyn Llydaw far below. There is a slight fall to the little col ahead and then a rise to the West Peak of Lliwedd, where the grand retrospect is worthy of attention as it is one of the most dramatic scenes on the Horseshoe. Still keeping to the edge of the cliffs, the well-marked track descends over tricky rock and boulders, and care is needed here as a slip on the R would be fatal. The path levels out on the approach to Bwlch y Saethau

Plate 22 **Route 3**

Plate 23 **Routes 2 and 3**

Plate 24 This scene is passed on L of **Route 3**

Plate 25 **Route 4**

Plate 26 Retrospect of **Route 4** from the West Peak

and is joined by the Watkin Path coming up on the L from Cwm-llan. The last section, rising diagonally over scree to Y Wyddfa, is the most trying part of this ascent, and while this most used track slants to the L across the shattered flanks of the peak to join the Rhyd Ddu path above Bwlch Main, some climbers prefer to make a direct attack upon it and emerge on the skyline on the east shoulder of Snowdon below the cairn, but this is not recommended as a line of descent owing to exposure and erosion.

Route 5. The Watkin Path. This popular ascent leaves the main road threading Nant Gwynant opposite the car park at Pont Bethania. A gate gives access to the resurfaced road leading to Hafod-llan farm, but after some 500 yards it bears L through the rhododendrons along the old miners' road and emerges above the stream coming down from Cwm-llan. A charming waterfall is passed on the R and above it an almost level stretch passes some derelict mine buildings on R, goes over a wooden bridge to Plas Cwm-llan also on R, and with a view high up on the L of the summit of Yr Aran. This one-time pleasant residence was used during the Second World War as a target for Commandos and is now an unsightly ruin. Thence the track passes close to the Gladstone Rock on L, where a tablet commemorates the opening of this path by Gladstone, then eighty-four years of age, on September 13th, 1892. The yawning mouth of Cwm-llan now opens up ahead and is entered by a shaly path leading to a deserted slate quarry, but turn sharp R before reaching the roofless buildings and climb steadily with Bwlch Main towering on L and Craig Ddu rising on R. A little rock gateway appears on the skyline ahead and this reveals the most shattered front of Snowdon, whence the path meanders round to the R and ultimately joins Route 4 on the crest of Bwlch y Saethau. The view from this pass comes as a surprise; for it discloses Glasyln below on L and the full length of Llyn Llydaw on R, between which a rough rock spur, known as Y Gribin, affords a nice scramble for those wishing to reach Route 3.

Plate 27 **Route 5**—A waterfall beside the Watkin Path

Plate 28 **Route 5**—Seen on emerging from the trees

Plate 29 **Route 5**—The ruins of Plas Cwm-llan

Plate 30 **Routes 5 and 6**

Plate 31 **Route 5**—Tablet on Gladstone Rock

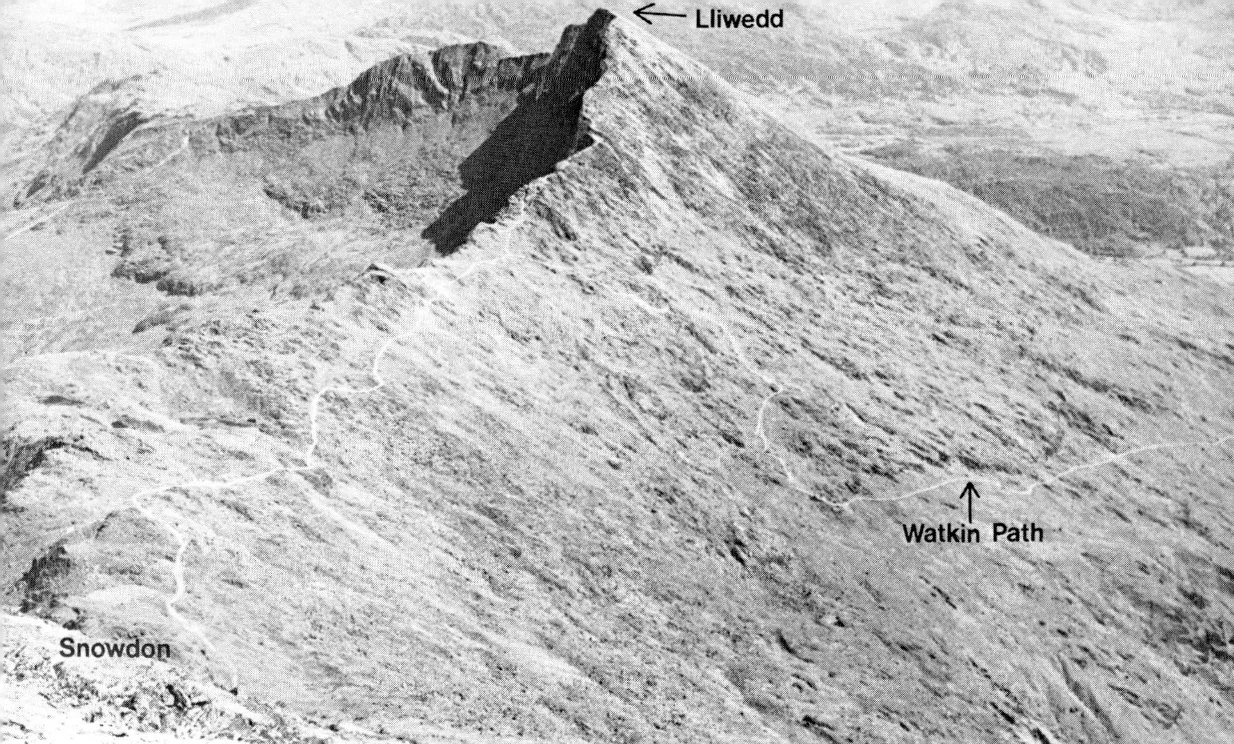

Plate 32 The terminal stretches of **Route 5**

Plate 33 **Route 6**—Yr Aran reflected in the calm surface of Llyn Gwynant

Route 6. Yr Aran and Bwlch Main. Follow Route 5 to Plas Cwm-llan but just before reaching it take the grassy path on the L which rises gently to cross the old mine railway line, bends L and R at an easy gradient and passes a derelict mine building on L before rising towards old mine workings on L (keep clear of these as there is no fence and the excavations are deep). Thence scramble up the grassy bank to the ridge where turn R and follow a dry stone wall along its crest, crossing it before the steepest section of the path rises to the summit cairn; it opens up splendid prospects in all directions; with a fine vista to the north-west of Mynydd Mawr and Llyn Cwellyn, and a grand view to the north-east of Moel Siabod, with a glimpse of Llyn Gwynant below. But the magnificent perspective of the South Ridge of Snowdon will rivet the gaze and its crest affords the final section of this route to Yr Wyddfa. There is at first a sharp descent to Bwlch Cwm-llan, where a rock-bound pool on the R and an almost round little tarn on the L will charm the eye. Thereafter the collar work begins: keep to the edge of the sharp drops on R and on attaining the saddle the Rhyd-ddu Path comes in on the L from Llechog, whence ascend the clearly marked track along the crest of the Bwlch Main to attain the cairn on the summit of the peak.

Route 7. Rhyd-ddu and Llechog. This easy ascent is one of the neglected delights of the group and incidentally most rewarding to photographers. There are two starting points: that nearest Beddgelert is favoured by pedestrians and the other, just outside the hamlet of Rhyd-ddu, is preferred by motorists because South Snowdon Station, on the long-disused Welsh Highland Railway, has been converted into a spacious car park and is quite close to the gate giving access to the main route. The key to the former is Pitt's Head on the Beddgelert–Caernarvon road. Turn R here for the sequestered farm of Ffridd-uchaf, easily recognised by its embowering shield of conifers; pass it on L and follow the grassy track until it merges with the quarry road coming up from Rhyd-

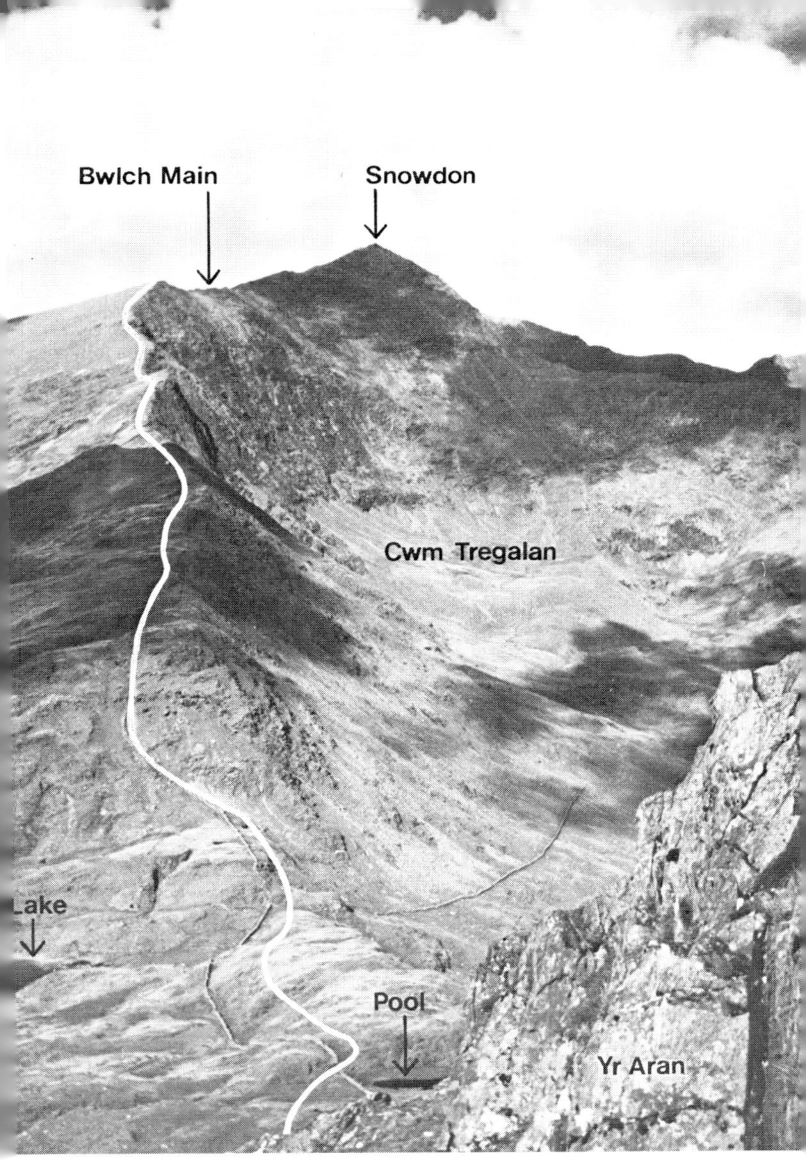

Plate 34 **Route 6**

Plate 35 **Route 6**—South-west from Yr Aran

Plate 36 **Route 6**—West from Yr Aran

Plate 37 **Route 6**—North-east from Yr Aran

Plate 38 Bwlch Main. Final stretch of **Routes 6 and 7**

ddu. The key to the latter is an iron gate from which the disused quarry road goes due east. Pass a deep quarry on R, conspicuous by the V-shaped opening in its far wall, and follow the road as it contours round the hillside until some bold rocks are encountered on L. This is a splendid viewpoint for the appraisal of Llyn Cwellyn, enclosed on L by Mynydd Mawr and on R by Foel Goch. A few steps ahead pass through another gate and circle the crag opposite for the next turn in the track which otherwise might be missed. This is an iron gate on L situated at the point of mergence with the Beddgelert track. Climbers who are familiar with this route could vary it by continuing along the old quarry road past the iron gate with fine views ahead of Yr Aran. This leads to the old South Snowdon mine buildings whence Bwlch Cwm-llan can be easily reached. Here turn L and follows Route 6 to the summit of Snowdon. The route now takes a direct line for Llechog, well seen on the skyline with Yr Wyddfa on R, and it winds its way uphill in and out of rocky outcrops, eventually to reach another gate in a substantial stone wall, with a large sheepfold on the other side. This is a good near-viewpoint for Yr Aran, and also for the many tops of the Moel Hebog range in the distant south-west. The path is unmistakable and soon crosses a level green clearing containing the ruin of a hut, long ago used as a place of refreshment, after which it rises more steeply over rock and scree ultimately to thread the boulders scattered in profusion on the broad crest of Llechog. This is a revealing coign of vantage, since its steep slabs fall into the vast basin of Cwm Clogwyn, embellished by several twinkling tarns, and on R to the conspicuous shoulder and serrated ridge of Bwlch Main. Farther to the R there is a grand array of the peaks crowning the Moel Hebog group, below which Llyn y Gadair and Llyn Cwellyn reflect the afternoon light. Now climb the broad stony track to the saddle and here join Route 6 for the summit of Snowdon, meanwhile enjoying the enchanting views on R of Cwm-llan and of Moel Siabod above Bwlch y Saethau.

Plate 39 Key to **Route 7**

Plate 40 Start of **Route 7** for walkers from Beddgelert

Plate 41 Early stage of **Route 7** from Rhyd-ddu

Plate 42 **Route 7**

Plate 43 **Route 7**—Seen from the point where the two tracks merge

Plate 44 Retrospect from **Route 7**

Plate 45 **Route 7**

Plate 46 Backward View of **Route 7**

Plate 47 Starting point of **Route 8**

Route 8. The Snowdon Ranger. This may well be the oldest route to Snowdon and is named after its first guide who may have lived in or near the present Youth Hostel which faces the rippling waters of Llyn Cwellyn. It yields a very pleasant approach to Yr Wyddfa and is seldom crowded, save on those rare occasions when the ardent youth hostellers invade it in force. Leave your car in the park opposite and start the ascent by crossing a stile to the L of the Hostel and make for the farm farther up the green hillside. Then zigzag through the pastures above it and go through a gate in a stone wall on top R. This gives access to a wide grassy path, with a wonderful retrospect of Mynydd Mawr and Llyn Cwellyn, and farther on of the Nantlle Ridge and Moel Hebog. Go through a small iron gate, round which sheep often congregate, and then tread the gradually rising moorland path, with a grand prospect ahead of Cwm Clogwyn, enclosed on L by the slopes of Clogwyn Du'r Arddu, on the R by the cliffs of Llechog, and dominated by Yr Wyddfa.

The well-trodden path passes below Bwlch Cwm-brwynog, but walk up to it on L and rest awhile to enjoy the fine retrospect of the Moel Hebog range on the other side of the valley. Then, instead of rejoining the path on R, keep to the crest of Clogwyn Du'r Arddu, and from a safe viewpoint look down its beetling precipices, which are the playground of the expert rock climber, to the stygian waters of Llyn Du'r Arddu, cradled in a wilderness of boulders at the foot of the crags. From the top of this eminence note the view of the Snowdon Railway near Clogwyn Station, backed by the shapely tops of the Glyders. Thereafter, return to the track on R and follow it to the summit of Snowdon, of which the section below the fork comes up from Llanberis.

Note—An alternative approach starts at Bron Fedw Isaf and is waymarked to join the original track higher up the hillside.

Plate 48 Retrospect from **Route 8**

Plate 49 View R of **Route 8**

Plate 50 View ahead of **Route 8**

Plate 51 **Route 8**

Plate 52 **Route 8**—Point of divergence

Plate 53 Bird's-eye view of Llyn Du'r Arddu from **Route 8**

Plate 54 Final stretch of **Route 8**, seen from Clogwyn Du'r Arddu

Route 9. The Llanberis Path. This is the longest, least arduous and most popular route to Snowdon; it involves a walk of about five miles over a gently graded path and at the Halfway House refreshments are obtainable, a boon much appreciated by climbers on a hot summer day. The key to this route is the Square at the end of the first side road above the Snowdon Railway Station, where a gate gives access to a mounting by-road, with the railway on R. This degenerates into a rough stony path, which may be rather damp after a wet spell, and on turning L it continues to rise, passes under the railway, and then levels out right up to the Halfway House. The majestic cliffs of Clogwyn Du'r Arddu are now revealed and they appear on R until the path rises above them after passing Clogwyn Station. Hereabouts is the real reward of the ascent; for by going over to the spur nearby the most dramatic view is obtained of the Llanberis Pass, far below and hemmed in by the steep slopes of Snowdon and the Glyders. Continuing the ascent, the path goes under the railway and keeps beside it and below the dome of Crib y Ddysgl, all the way to the end of the line, whence the large cairn just above the hotel crowning Yr Wyddfa is quickly attained.

Warning. Although Route 9 is the easiest ascent of Snowdon, winter conditions can transform it into one of the most dangerous. For in deep snow the path disappears and climbers tend to keep to the railway or what can be seen of it. The most dangerous section is between Clogwyn Station and Bwlch Glas, where a shelf carries the line which fills up with snow that lasts most of the winter. It becomes hard and icy and very difficult to traverse safely. And since several fatal accidents have occurred here every climber should avoid it at all costs.

Plate 55 Distant view of **Route 9** from Llyn Padarn

Plate 56 Railway and **Route 9** run side by side

Plate 57 Llanberis Pass, seen from Clogwyn Station

Plate 58 **Route 9**

Route 10. Cwm Glas. This sporting route is seldom used, save by the connoisseur who can revel in the solitude and wild grandeur of Cwm Glas, which is decked with Alpine flora in the spring and graced by a lovely tarn that opens up a surprising view of the Glyders. Follow Route 1 to the sheepfold and then bear R over a grassy shoulder to a small cairn that is the only sure key to the path. This is well cairned but rather indistinct in places, contours round the slopes below Bwlch y Moch, and then ascends over stony ground to a cairn perched on the northern spur of Crib Goch, above Dinas Mot. The cwm is now revealed on L and is enclosed by mural precipices in which the Parson's Nose, a prominent cliff beloved by rock climbers, is centrally situated. The path skirts the western flanks of the spur and then continues along a grassy shelf, to end where the stream falls from Llyn Glas. A short step uphill brings it into view, and on its far side a level green stretch makes a good camping ground for climbers. This is a remote and delightful spot in which to soliloquise on a warm sunny day; for the rocky shelf holding the lake in its grip cuts off all sound of traffic in Llanberis Pass below, and the only sign of life is the occasional climber wending his way across the lofty ridge of Crib Goch on the southern wall of the cwm.

There are two exits that join Route 1: the first and easiest is to walk up beside the stream feeding the tarn in the direction of the Pinnacles, and then to climb the scree on R to Bwlch Coch; the second is to go R of the Parson's Nose, pass a tiny pool cupped in bare rock, and then to ascend the steep scree that emerges on the skyline near the summit of Crib y Ddysgl. In both cases Route 1 is followed to the summit of Snowdon.

Plate 50. **Route 10** begins at this point on **Routes 1 and 2**

Plate 60 **Route 10**

Plate 61 First view of Cwm Glas from **Route 10**

Plate 62 **Route 10**—First exit

Plate 63 **Route 10**—Second exit

The Glyders group

Glyder Fawr	3,279 feet	999 metres
Glyder Fach	3,262 feet	994 metres
Y Garn	3,104 feet	946 metres
Elidir Fawr	3,029 feet	924 metres
Tryfan	3,010 feet	917 metres
Foel Goch	2,726 feet	831 metres
Carnedd y Filiast	2,694 feet	821 metres
Mynydd Perfedd	2,664 feet	812 metres
Nameless Peak	2,636 feet	803 metres
Bwlch Caseg-fraith	2,588 feet	788 metres
Elidir Fach	2,564 feet	782 metres
Esgair Felen	2,500 feet	762 metres
Gallt yr Ogof	2,499 feet	762 metres
Bwlch Tryfan	2,350 feet	716 metres

When seen from the south and west, the range of hills dominated by Glyder Fawr looks comparatively uninteresting as it merely displays a succession of vast grassy slopes interspersed here and there with outcropping rocks that are crowned by the sharp little top of the Castle of the Winds. The only notable exception is that of the single spur of Esgair Felen, whose reddish broken cliffs catch the eye and overhang the craggy declivities confined to this one point on this side of the group, bordered by the Llanberis Pass.

But when seen from the north this aspect changes dramatically and comes as a complete surprise; for one savage cwm follows another from east to west, all of them hemmed in by striking mural precipices. The range is further enhanced by the beautiful isolated peak of Tryfan, and amid the whole stands Ogwen Cottage, the hub of the many ascents from this side of the group.

Mynydd Perfedd
Bwlch-y-Brecan
Foel Goch
Llyn Cywion
Pont Pen-y-benglog
Maes Caradoc
Tŷ-gwyn
Braich-du
Craig-ddu
1044m
Llyn Ogwen
Falls
303m
YH
Y Garn
Llyn-y-Cŵn
Devil's Kitchen
Glyder Fawr
999m
Esgair
Afon Las
Llanberis
A 4086
Pass of Llanberis
Pont-y-Gromlech
Llyn Cwm Ffynnon
Y Foel Berfedd
356m
Crib Goch
Pen-y-Pass
Nature Trail
921m
Llyn Glas
Cwm Glas
923m
831m
821m
Filiast
Dudodyn
11
12
13
14
15
16
22
23
24
24a
25
26

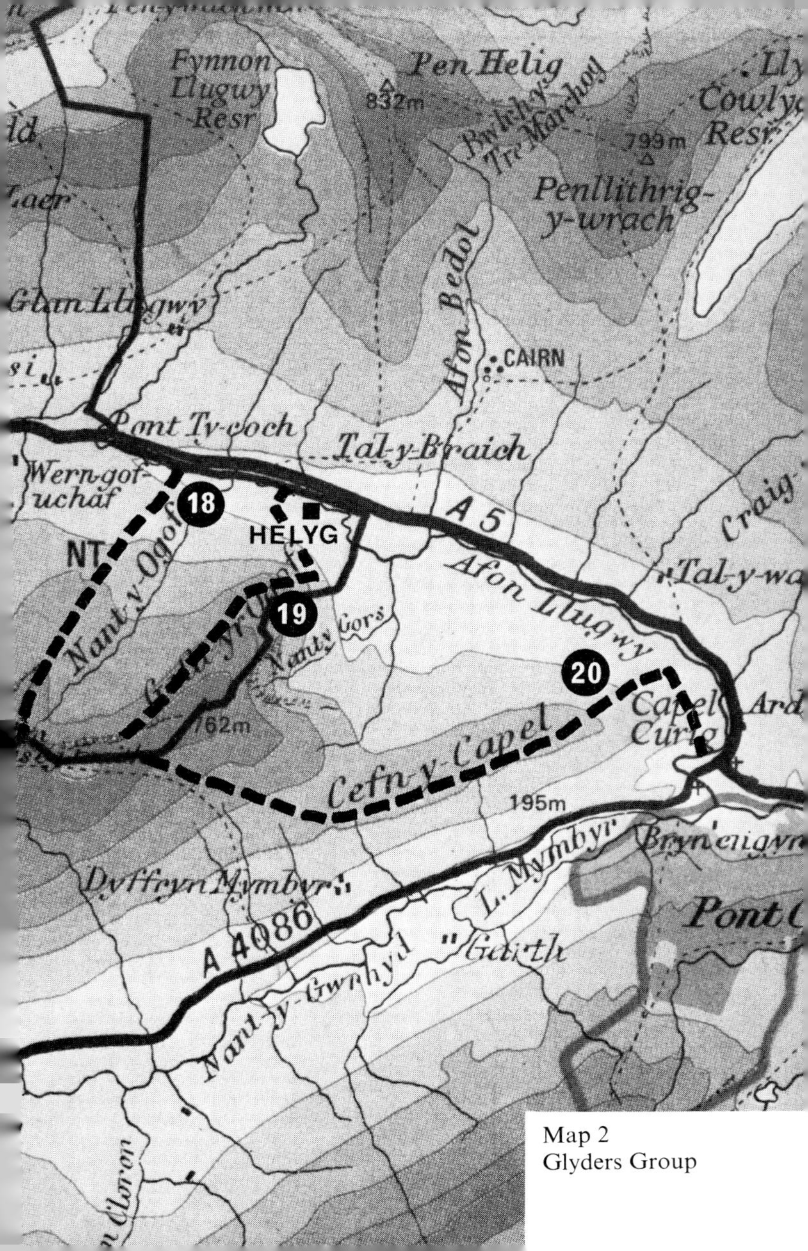

Map 2
Glyders Group

Moreover, the summit ridge of the Glyders is unique in Wales and characterised by a grand display of chaotically arranged boulders whose desolate aspect vies with that of the main ridge of the Coolins, in the Misty Isle of Skye, for pride of place in wild Britain.

In view of these remarkable features it is not to be wondered at that the range draws legions of climbers, and there are so many routes up and over the group that many days can be spent in their exploration. All the important ascents are dealt with in the following pages, any or all of which may be climbed by persons in fit and vigorous condition. In snow, even on a clear day, climbing in the Glyders requires the utmost care when Alpine experience is a decided advantage.

Glyder Fawr

Route 11. Ogwen Cottage and the Devil's Kitchen. Now that the new road beside Llyn Ogwen has been completed, motorists have a choice of three car parks from which to ascend any of the adjacent routes. There is one below the Milestone Buttress, another half way to Ogwen Cottage and a commodious third between the Cottage and Youth Hostel. And it is here that this newly constructed route begins, and later on keeps well above the marshy ground to eventually turn sharp R for Llyn Idwal. Pass the gate now the boundary of the Cwm Idwal National Nature Reserve, which opens up a revealing view of the first section of the route ahead, with the great cleft of the Devil's Kitchen on the skyline. Keep the lake R, pass Idwal Slabs L, and ascend the well-marked path which bears R and eventually threads the immense boulders below the Kitchen. The retrospect from the mouth of the cavern is magnificent, with Llyn Idwal below, Llyn Ogwen in the middle distance and the Carneddau in the background, dominated by the shattered front of Pen y Ole Wen. Now turn L and climb the steep, boulder-strewn shelf to the skyline where a prominent cairn marks the route. Continue ahead towards Llyn-y-Cwn R and mount the twisting scree path

Plate 64 The enlarged Ogwen Cottage—starting point of **Routes 11–15**, and **25–26**, also **33**

which ultimately emerges on the broad summit of Glyder Fawr. This is one of the most desolate spots in Snowdonia, and a peculiarly shaped eminence of slate dominates this rocky top of the highest peak of the group.

The panorama from this stony wilderness is extensive, but restricted by the plateau-like top of the mountain. The view to the east along its wide ridge may first catch the eye, since its forlorn aspect suggests what might well be the surface of the moon. The Castle of the Winds appears below the great heap of stones that characterise Glyder Fach, about a mile distant on L, of which rises the summit of Tryfan. To the south Snowdon and Crib Goch present a serrated skyline, and to the west Mynydd Mawr tops the ridge enclosing the Llanberis Pass, while to the north the vast bulk of the Carneddau stretches away in the distance, crowned by the prominent summits of Carnedds Ddafydd and Llywelyn. This coign of vantage stands at the head of four valleys, but to see them on a clear day involves a stroll round the rim of the plateau. They are: Nant Ffrancon to the Menai Straits; the Conway Valley to the sea near the Great Orme; Nant Gwynant to Harlech and the sea; and Llanberis Pass to Caernarvon.

When this Route is used for the descent to Ogwen, it is worth while to pick up the stream from Llyn-y-Cwn and to follow it to the Devil's Kitchen, see plate 102, whence the path may be regained by crossing the grassy hummocks.

Route 12. Cwm Idwal and the Nameless Cwm. Follow Route 11 to Idwal Slabs, but bear L up the grassy slopes before reaching them. When the Nameless Cwm opens up R, ascend the ridge above Idwal Slabs to the skyline, whence turn R and walk up to the cairns on Glyder Fawr.

Plate 65 **Route 11**—Idwal Slabs

Plate 66 **Route 11**

Plate 67 Last stretch of **Route 11**

Plate 68 Eastern prospect from Glyder Fawr

Plate 69 **Route 12**

Route 13. The Gribin. Leave Ogwen Cottage by Route 11, and do not desert it until the gate is reached, whence turn L and later R to climb the grassy slopes of the Gribin. A most interesting approach is to follow Route 11 almost as far as Idwal Slabs and to then climb L up the steep grassy slopes which terminate on the lower section of the ridge. This variation has the element of surprise, in that on attaining the crest of the Gribin, Tryfan and Llyn Bochlwyd are suddenly revealed to the east, where the blue of the lake, surrounded by its green carpet of grass, contrasts strongly with the pale stony declivities of the mountain. The ridge rises gently at first over grass, with glimpses R of the Devil's Kitchen and Y Garn, and eventually changes abruptly to rock. Climb carefully until its top is attained and then stride confidently ahead towards the disintegrated slabs of the Castle of the Winds, which fall L precipitously into the cwm. Turn R on the ridge, pass the forlorn hollow of the Nameless Cwm R, and follow the path through the stones and strange collections of crags to the summit of Glyder Fawr.

Plate 70 **Route 13**

Plate 71 **Routes 14 and 15** Seen from The Gribin

Plate 72 **Route 13** Seen from Tryfan

Plate 73 **Route 13** Top of the Gribin

Plate 74 **Routes 14 and 15**

Route 14. Llyn Bochlwyd, Bristly Ridge and Glyder Fach. Follow Route 13 beyond the Gribin turnoff and a little further on bear R and then go straight ahead by the line of cairns to the stream coming down from Llyn Bochlwyd. Climb beside it until this sombre lake comes into view and rest awhile by its shore to contemplate its wild situation. It is enclosed L by Tryfan and R by the Gribin, while ahead rise the cliffs supporting Glyder Fach which are a favourite playground for the rock climber. Proceed by keeping the lake R and tread the gradually rising path which bears L by this wedge-shaped mountain and R by Bristly Ridge. Pass the stone wall and turn R where the route to the ridge is plainly visible since it bears the nailmarks of thousands of climbers who have passed this way. On reaching the base of the crags the track rises steeply and twists in and out of buttress and pinnacle, clearly marked throughout and quite safe for those with a steady head, to emerge finally on the broad stony ridge. Now turn R and go over to inspect the Cantilever L, a great slab poised securely on vertical crags, whose top may be reached by an easy scramble. Then continue ahead to Glyder Fach L whose massive pile of boulders is a conspicuous landmark hereabouts. Scramble to the top if you feel like it, but be careful, and then go over to the Castle of the Winds, with L a fine prospect of Snowdon and R a view of the gradually rising plateau ending at Glyder Fawr. It is better to climb straight over the Castle rather than take the circuitous course L round its base, and descend carefully through the maze of vertical slabs of slate on its far side. Walk down to the col and there join Route 13 for the summit of the reigning peak of the group.

Plate 75 **Route 14**—Llyn Bochlwyd

Plate 76 Retrospect from **Route 14**

Plate 77 **Route 14**—The Cantilever

Plate 78 **Route 14**—Glyder Fach

Plate 79 **Route 14**

Route 15. Ogwen Cottage and Tryfan Scree Gully. Follow Route 14 to the stream but do not ascend the path beside it. Continue L and pick up the track which rises steeply R, first over grass and finally by a conspicuous scree gully that emerges on the summit of Tryfan. This arduous route is not recommended.

Route 16. The North Ridge of Tryfan. This is one of the most interesting and entertaining scrambles in all Wales and the usual starting point is near the head of Llyn Ogwen, but the lower shoulder of the mountain may also be reached by a direct ascent from the other side of the ridge. Go through a gate L of the Milestone Buttress and climb the long twisting staircase that first mounts beside a wall R and later in the shadow of the Buttress itself. The track emerges on the shoulder which is covered with deep heather and has a cairn marking the meeting of several paths; it might even be called the Piccadilly Circus of Tryfan for tracks radiate and rise sharply up the North Ridge, the alternative approach from the east comes in, and it is the point of departure for Heather Terrace which rises diagonally across the eastern flanks of the peak at the foot of its three prominent buttresses. This landmark may be avoided by climbers who do not object to the ascent of a long scree slope, for one goes up from the bend in the track below this cairn. Thence there are so many variations in the route to the next shoulder that it is a matter of personal taste as to which of them is chosen, but that centrally situated can be most easily followed. Many parts of it are steep and slippery, and there are a few tricky bits where a conveniently placed handhold assists the passage. It rises diagonally R round speculative corners and past the "Cannon", a huge leaning rock that is well seen from Ogwen, until eventually the second shoulder is attained. This platform calls for a halt, if only to scan the horizon which has widened enormously as height was gained. At this stage perhaps the most striking prospect is that of Llyn Ogwen, now far below, which even on sunny days looks black and forbidding against

Plate 80 Start of **Route 16**

Tryfan
Bwlch Tryfan

Plate 82 View R of **Route 16**

its brightly coloured engirdling hill slopes.

Ahead rises the last obstacle in this sporting course and since it consists entirely of rock it is best to tackle it direct from the point where the track ends against the cliff. However, there is an alternative L, where a faint path leads into the North Gully which is jammed with boulders and slabs to afford an enclosed variation to the other more exposed route. Both of them emerge on the North Peak, and it is only a short step to Adam and Eve, the two conspicuous upturned boulders that crown the summit of Tryfan.

On a sunny day it is usual to find a number of climbers gathered round this lofty perch; for it is a pleasant spot on which to eat lunch, to tackle the spectacular and risky "step" from Adam to Eve and to enjoy the spacious panorama. The vista R and L along the valley extending from Capel Curig to Bethesda is of course attractive and divided by Llyn Ogwen far below. It is bounded on the north by the vast green slopes of the Carneddau whose broad ridges culminate in Carnedd Llywelyn. But their smooth flanks do not attract the eye so strongly as the immediate landscape of the Glyders themselves, where Llyn Idwal and Llyn Bochlwyd sparkle on the floor of the rockbound cwms stretching westwards. Bristly Ridge forms a broken wedge to the south, and the eye wanders R over the ridge to the crags supporting the Gribin, passing centrally the very tip of Snowdon which will be missed even on a clear day by those who do not possess an alert and discerning eye! Farther R the skyline rises gently to Glyder Fawr, and then after a fall to the Devil's Kitchen rises again to Y Garn and continues westwards in an almost flat line to Foel Goch, above which the curving ridge of Elidir Fawr will draw the eye. Thence it passes over Mynydd Perfedd, finally to merge with the rising slopes of Pen yr Ole Wen.

There is still a long way to go to Glyder Fawr and in consequence the climber must not linger too long on his airy seat; so begin the descent by crossing the crest that leads to the South Peak and glance back at the summit of Tryfan to grasp more clearly its isolated situation. Then carefully

Plate 83 **Route 16**—Adam and Eve

descend the twisting track which passes in and out of gaps between the boulders and eventually reaches a little col separating the main peak from its shapely satellite, on top of which L lies a charming rock-bound pool reflecting the colour of the sky. Now bear R and wander down the clearly marked path to Bwlch Tryfan, there to join Route 14 to the crowning peak of the group.

Plate 84 **Route 16** West from Tryfan

Route 17. Heather Terrace. If you come by car, park it at the farmhouse of Gwern-y-Gof-Uchaf, which stands back from the road L just above the head of Llyn Ogwen, and clearly reveals Heather Terrace as a diagonal line rising across the face of Tryfan. Leave the back of the farm and pass L some inclined slabs which are used as a practice ground by rock climbers. Then join the path R which crosses some marshy ground and later rises over scree to the cairn noted in Route 16. Now proceed in and out of a collection of boulders that stand amid thick heather and bilberries to gain the Terrace, which follow upwards past the base of the three buttresses and their adjacent gullies, all of which rise into the sky right up to the summit of Tryfan and afford one of the most treasured playgrounds of the rock climber. Bear R at the termination of the Terrace and go over a low stone wall to the col, at which point join Route 16 for the remainder of the ascent.

Route 18. Bwlch Caseg-fraith. The ridge rising to this pass from the Ogwen Valley is one of the most revealing and least used in this group of hills. It is a paradise for the photographer, and as long ago as 1941 I gave an account of it in my *Snowdonia through the Lens*, when a friend came with me from Helyg to Pen y Pass over the Glyders in superb Alpine conditions. Yet, although I have since ascended it on several occasions I have never encountered another climber or photographer with whom I could share the rare beauty of the magnificent scenes it unfolds.

The key to this route is the farmhouse of Gwern-y-Gof-Isaf, which nestles at the very root of the ridge on the south side of the Afon Llugwy, almost opposite Helyg, and is reached by crossing a picturesque bridge from the main highway. Those who come by car may park the vehicle near the farm. The ridge rises in grassy steps, interspersed with crags which become more plentiful as height is gained; it is enclosed R by Cwm Tryfan and L by Nant yr Ogof. About half-way along its crest there is a grand prospect of Tryfan across the cwm, and from this height the peak assumes its true elevation and

Plate 85 **Route 17** Seen from Helyg

under snow assumes the splendour of an Alpine giant. The ridge steepens and later flattens out on a lofty plateau rimmed with crags, on which repose Llyn Caseg-fraith and two smaller pools. They are priceless gems in a sombre setting, and on a calm day reflect the upper buttresses of Tryfan to perfection. There is also a splendid view of Bristly Ridge L, whose pinnacles and buttresses are clearly delineated by the sunlight before noon. A rather indistinct track threads the soft marshy ground hereabouts, and on leaving the platform it swings R and crosses the Miners' Track coming up from Pen-y-gwryd and going over to Bwlch Tryfan beneath the crags of Bristly Ridge. Thereafter it skirts the rim of Cwm Tryfan and eventually joins Route 14 at the top of Bristly Ridge.

Route 19. Gallt yr Ogof. This rounded craggy eminence is the first of the Glyder group to come into view L when proceeding westwards along the Holyhead road from Capel Curig. It may be reached conveniently by walking along the old road from this village where a car may be parked. But a nearer approach by the motorist, if he happens to be a member of the Climbers' Club, is to leave the vehicle in the park opposite Helyg and use the public footpath nearby, cross the Afon Llugwy by a footbridge and turn L to walk the shorter distance to the crag, whence a nice scramble up a conspicuous diagonal gully places him on the skyline. Here you turn L for the summit and then bear R for the Nameless Peak whose far side slopes down to Llyn Caseg-fraith. Here you join Route 18 for Glyder Fawr.

Plate 86 **Route 18**—Buttresses of Tryfan

Plate 87 Starting point of **Route 18**

Plate 88 Tryfan from **Route 18**—Bwlch Caseg-fraith

Plate 89 Bristly Ridge seen from **Route 18**

Plate 90 Llyn Caseg-fraith—Retrospect from **Route 18**

Plate 91 **Route 19**—Gallt yr Ogof from the Holyhead Road

Plate 92 **Route 19**

Route 20. The Ridge from Capel Curig. The long and lofty ridge of this group begins almost at the very doors of the village and its complete traverse, followed by the descent from Glyder Fawr to Ogwen Cottage, requires good weather and a long day. The best approach to it is by the lane L of the post office. Cross the bridge with the noisy cataract R and follow the old Ogwen road to the derelict barn beyond the last cottage whence bear L along the rising path until the higher ground is attained. If a direct line along its crest is taken several craggy eminences will be encountered, and it may be desirable to turn them on L or R. In due course pass round the rim of Nant y Gors R and make for the Nameless Peak to join Route 19 for the remainder of the long tramp.

Plate 93 **Route 20** goes along the ridge from Capel Curig

Route 21. Pen-y-gwryd and the Miners' Track. This popular path begins at a stile below the hotel and at a bend in the road opposite Llyn Lockwood. It takes a more or less direct line for the end of a stone wall running uphill R, which is reached after crossing the stream coming down over bare slabs from Llyn Cwmffynnon. The ground hereabouts is very boggy and even when climbing beside the wall several very wet patches are encountered. These terminate on passing through a gap in a cross wall, near a sharp corner L. Thence a cairned track slants uphill R through rock and heather, and at the end of this steep section it is worthwhile to look back at the fine vista down the Vale of Gwynant, and R to the Snowdon Horseshoe. Now continue the ascent at an easier gradient, past a waterfall L until a break in the rock ridge overhead gives access to vast areas of marshy ground on the summit plateau. Go forward until Llyn Caseg-fraith appears ahead. Here join Route 18 to Glyder Fawr L, or if proceeding to Ogwen Cottage follow the well-marked track that contours round the head of Cwm Tryfan, below the crags of Bristly Ridge.

Plate 94 Vale of Gwynant from **Route 21**

Plate 95 The Glyders from Pen-y-gwyrd

Plate 96 Starting point of **Routes 21** and **22**

Route 22. Pen-y-gwryd and Llyn Cwmffynnon. This is the most direct route from the south to the reigning peak of the group. Cross the stile below Pen-y-Gwryd and walk uphill L to reach the outflow of the lake. Continue R round its shore and on reaching the stream entering it from the Glyders walk by its banks and take the L branch which rises through the wide opening of Heather Gully. The going is very rough but not as steep as it looks from afar, and the route terminates quite suddenly by the cairns on Glyder Fawr. If the main stream is followed it will lead to the col below the Castle of the Winds, but by bearing L on reaching the grassy slopes and later R the summit of Glyder Fawr may be attained.

Route 23. Pen y Pass and Esgair Felen. Walk round the western end of the Youth Hostel and cross the wall by a stile. Ascend either the well marked stony track or bear L uphill over grass, and on reaching the skyline it opens up a comprehensive view of Llyn Cwmffynnon and the Glyders. Turn L up the long grassy shoulder of Glyder Fawr, past a remarkably perched boulder L, and when near the top of the slope bear L for the conspicuous red precipitous crags of Esgair Felen. This is a magnificent coign of vantage for the appraisal of the Crib Goch–Crib y Ddysgl section of the Horseshoe, for the view into Cwm Glas opposite with the stream falling steeply to the pass below, and for the long vista down the Llanberis Pass to the twin lakes at Llanberis. Then turn round and ascend the broad ridge that terminates on the summit of Glyder Fawr.

Plate 97 **Route 22**

Plate 98 **Route 23** Llanberis Pass from Esgair Felen

Plate 99 Terminal stretches of **Route 23**

Route 24. Nant Peris and Llyn y Cwn. Go to the bus stop at Gwastadnant in the Llanberis Pass which is about three-quarters of a mile above the church in Nant Peris, and there turn L along the stony walled path. This passes a white cottage and then goes through a small gate beside a larger one to follow the wall on the L towards a second cottage. Here a wooden stile gives access to a waymarked path which crosses a field to the Afon Las. Now turn R and ascend the steep L bank of the stream and higher up cross a second stile. Keep to the wall running uphill for some seventy yards, then take a diagonal course to the R where the eroded track appears ahead. Keep to the R of the cascading stream and also the waterfall on the skyline, whence the gradient becomes easier and is well cairned through Cwm Cneifio where boggy ground leads straight to Llyn y Cwn. Here turn R and ascend the final stages of Route 11 to Glyder Fawr.

If you are bound for Ogwen Cottage by the latter route, it is worth while to first bear L beyond the tarn and pick up the stream that leads to the Devil's Kitchen, and there observe the striking view of Llyn Idwal and Llyn Ogwen through the vertical walls of the chasm. Do not attempt to descend the Kitchen which is the strict preserve of the properly equipped rock climber.

It is essential that all walkers adhere strictly to this route as it was closed some time ago and only recently reopened and waymarked by the National Park warden service.

Plate 100 **Route 24** from Gwastadnant

of the waterfall

Plate 102 **Route 24** Looking down the Devil's Kitchen

Elidir Fawr

This peak is one of the more westerly of the Glyders group and presents a fine wedge shaped elevation when seen from Carnedd Llywelyn. It is often climbed from Ogwen by way of Y Garn when the distance to be covered is almost ten miles, whereas if ascended from Nant Peris it is considerably less. This new approach has received some attention by the Warden Service, due to the popularity of Elidir Fawr as one of the fourteen peaks, of which details are as follows:

Route 24a. Nant Peris and Elidir Fawr. When coming down the Llanberis Pass, turn R just beyond the Nant Peris Post Office by a chapel and follow the tarmacked road which rises gently round to the L to a white gate. Pass through it and continue along the cart track leading to Fron Farm, but just before reaching a second gate, embowered by four gigantic holly trees, break over a field to the R up to a wall and the stile set over it. A stone barn appears ahead and the path goes through a gate on its R and then begins to zig-zag over grass to gain height. Around the 800 feet contour it bears L and takes a gently rising line into Cwm Dudolyn on the R which is a public right of way. But on reaching an iron footbridge over the chattering Afon Dudolyn you cross it and the real collar work begins. It is a stiff climb all the way to the summit of Elidir Fawr, and to facilitate the crossing of a high mountain wall higher up its grassy slopes, it is proposed to erect one stile at G.R.607602 and another 400 yards to the R at G.R.609602. This lofty coign of vantage opens up a wide panorama round the western arc, and includes Anglesey and unusual prospects of the Snowdon Range.

Plate 103 **Route 24a** starts from the gate to Fron Farm

Plate 104 **Route 24a**—Retrospect from the zig-zags: Fron Farm on the R

Plate 105 **Route 24a**—The footbridge in Cwm Dudolyn where the collar work begins!

Y Garn and Foel Goch

Route 25. Ogwen Cottage and Llyn Clyd. These two mountains make a picturesque backdrop to the western prospect from the head of Llyn Ogwen, and when seen by morning light a dark shadow is cast into the wild cwm immediately below the summit of Y Garn, in which repose, out of sight from this viewpoint, the small tarn of Llyn Clyd and a placid pool just above it. The direct ascent of this peak is tough and unyielding, and there are two well-defined tracks: the fishermen's route is if anything less steep and rises L of the stream to end at Llyn Clyd; the climbers' route is some distance R and takes a direct line for the grassy ridge hemming in the cwm.

Follow Route 11 to Llyn Idwal and bear R along its shore. Pass round a boggy hollow and then ascend one or other of the alternative tracks already mentioned. Keep to the well-trodden path which rises along the crest of the ridge all the way to the cairn on Y Garn, and meanwhile note the wild prospect of the cwm below L. The isolated summit of Y Garn is a grand viewpoint and to the south unfolds a grim prospect of Snowdon and its satellites, with R views of Llanberis and the sea on a clear day. But it is the Glyders themselves that will hold the gaze, for their rocky cwms are disclosed to perfection across the void. Tryfan and Llyn Ogwen will catch the eye to the east and the riven declivities of Pen yr Ole Wen on the other side of Nant Ffrancon to the north contrast strangely with the smooth green slopes of the Carneddau in the background. Now walk in a north-westerly direction and keep to the rim of the cwm R all the way to Foel Goch, whose cairn is scarcely as revealing as that of Y Garn. This tramp, together with the return descent, is enough for the average pedestrian's day, but strong walkers should continue along the lofty ridge to Mynydd Perfedd which opens up a striking prospect of Elidir Fawr L, with Marchlyn Mawr R. Those bound for Llanberis may traverse this peak and descend to Nant Peris by Route 24a.

Plate 106 **Route 25**—Y Garn from Llyn Ogwen—alternative starts

However, climbers who wish to shorten the route may descend direct to the valley from Foel Goch by way of Esgair y Ceunant where a stile has now been erected over the high mountain wall.

Route 26. Ogwen Cottage and the Devil's Kitchen. Follow Route 25 to the boggy hollow and pick up the track L that skirts Llyn Idwal with splendid views of Idwal Slabs L. Then continue its ascent through the boulders to the Kitchen, and bear L to climb the shelf which emerges on the Llyn y Cwn plateau. Here turn R and scale the grassy slopes of Y Garn, and on encountering craggy ground glance down to Llyn Clyd before attaining the cairn on the summit of this peak.

Plate 107 **Route 25**—Wild Cwm on Y Garn

Plate 108 Retrospect from **Route 25**

Plate 109 **Route 25**—Snowdon from Y Garn

Plate 110 **Route 25**—The Glyders from Y Garn

Plate 111 **Route 25** Seen from Y Garn

Plate 112 **Route 26**

Plate 113 Idwal Slabs from **Route 26**

The Carneddau

Carnedd Llywelyn	3,484 feet	1,062 metres
Carnedd Ddafydd	3,426 feet	1,044 metres
Pen yr Ole Wen	3,210 feet	979 metres
Foel Grach	3,195 feet	974 metres
Craig Llugwy	3,184 feet	970 metres
Yr Elen	3,152 feet	961 metres
Foel Fras	3,091 feet	942 metres
Yr Aryg	2,875 feet	866 metres
Llwytmor	2,749 feet	838 metres
Pen yr Helgi-du	2,732 feet	833 metres
Penllithrig-y-wrach	2,621 feet	799 metres
Drum	2,528 feet	771 metres
Craig Eigiau	2,389 feet	709 metres
Creigiau Gleision	2,214 feet	675 metres
Pen y Castell	2,034 feet	620 metres
Tal-y-fan	2,000 feet	610 metres
Clogwyn Mawr	1,500 feet	457 metres

The Carneddau comprise the largest group of hills in Snowdonia and consist mainly of broad grassy ridges, scantily interspersed with outcrops of rocks, save the well-known cliffs of Craig yr Ysfa, Black Ladders and the steep shattered southern front of Pen yr Ole Wen.

They afford excellent walking country, free from major problems, but the distances to be covered in their exploration are misleading to the eye, and, moreover, the vast plateau-like summit of Carnedd Llywelyn is one of the mistiest spots in the group.

In extremely bad conditions climbers may go on to the small stone shelter built by the Warden Service fifty yards north east of the nearby Foel Grach summit. Moreover, in this immense area it is easy to get lost in bad weather, and I therefore advise all climbers to descend by one or other of the routes described herein if they wish to reach the valley safely.

The enormous whale-back ridges, though in places well cairned, can be difficult in mist owing to the absence of well-defined landmarks, and in bad weather walks should be confined to the ascent of one or other of the peaks within easy reach of the Ogwen Valley. To make a successful traverse of the range in these conditions requires expert use of map and compass, together with long experience of the group as a whole, but on clear days no difficulties should be encountered.

The following routes include most of the popular ascents, but in view of the vast distances from the well-known centres of the most northerly tops they have been omitted from this work.

Unhappily, however, it will come as a great surprise and disappointment to all climbers bound for Craig yr Ysfa when they find this cherished wilderness has been invaded by the Central Electricity Generating Board. For they have replaced the old straight track from Helyg which penetrated into the heart of the Carneddau by a new road that ends at the dam constructed at Ffynnon Llugwy. The purpose of this 2½ kilometer road is to service the new reservoir which will replace the water supply from Marchlyn Mawr; a part of the Dinorwic Pump Storage Scheme. This piece of vandalism in the Snowdonia National Park will always be an eyesore to every lover of this delectable part of Wales.

Map 3
Carneddau—South

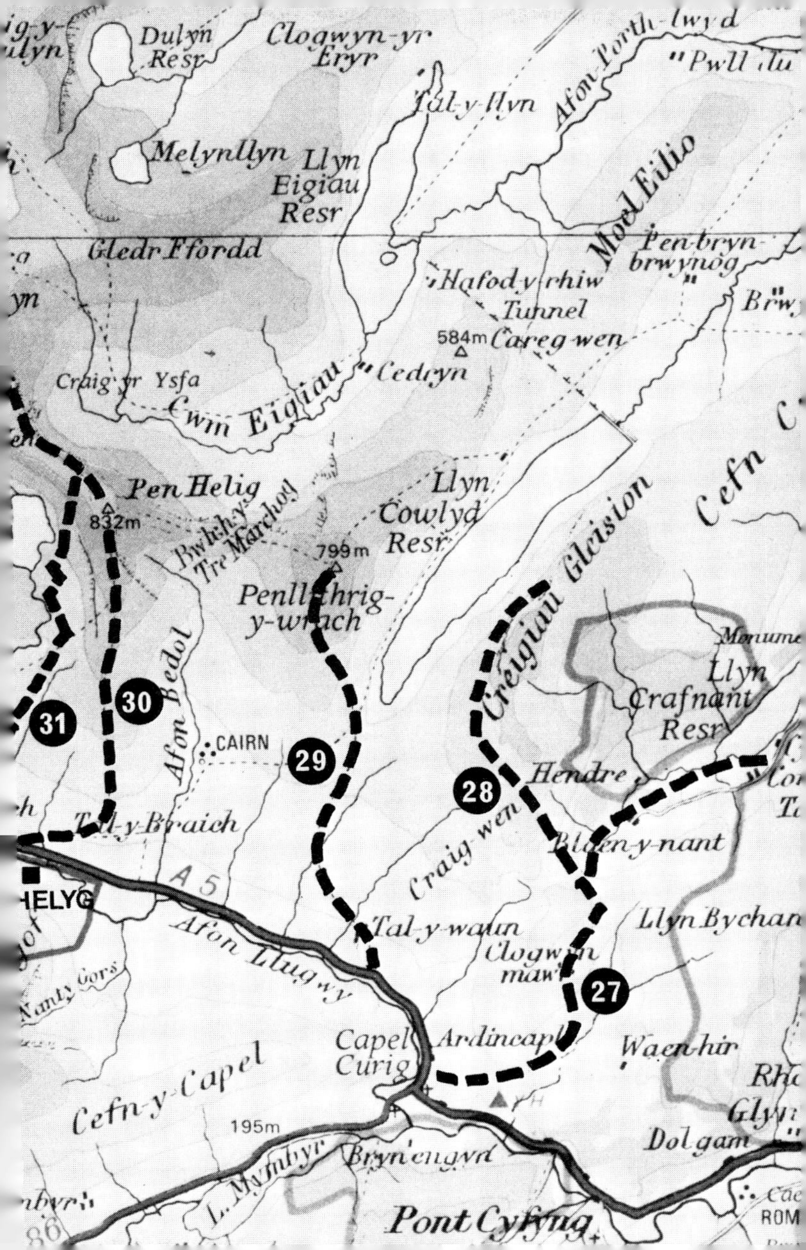
Dulyn Resr
Clogwyn-yr Eryr
Afon Porth-lwyd
Tal-y-llyn
Melynllyn
Llyn Eigiau Resr
Moel Eilio
Gledr Ffordd
Pen-bryn-brwynog
Hafod-y-rhiw
Tunnel
584m
Careg wen
Craig yr Ysfa
Cedcyn
Cwm Eigiau
Pen Helig
832m
Bwlch-y-Tre Marchog
Llyn Cowlyd Resr
799m
Penllithrig-y-wrach
Creigiau Gleision
Cefn
Llyn Crafnant Resr
Afon Bedol
CAIRN
31
30
29
28
27
Hendre
Tal-y-Braich
Craig wen
Blaen-y-nant
A5
HELYG
Tal-y-waun
Llyn Bychan
Afon Llugwy
Clogwyn mawr
Nant-y-Gors
Capel Curig
Ardincaple
Waen-hir
Cefn-y-Capel
YH
195m
Dolgam
L. Mymbyr
Bryn'engwd
Pont Cyfyng
ROM

Route 27. Llyn Crafnant and Clogwyn Mawr. The easy walk to this lovely lake through a charming wild valley is one of the delights enjoyed by every visitor who stays in Capel Curig, and if desired may include Llyn Geirionnydd on the return journey. However, the former may also be reached by car from Trefriw and the latter by driving sharp L at the Ugly House. Hence, by combining walking with riding this enchanting corner of the Carneddau can be seen with the minimum of effort.

The route for pedestrians leaves Capel by the stile opposite the post office. Follow the path past the conspicuous Pinnacles R, then cross a stream where the ground is often damp, and go through another gate into some woods at the foot of a rocky eminence L. On emerging from the trees walk over the flat stones laid throughout in damp places, then cross another stream and continue uphill at an easy gradient until the valley comes into view ahead. Now pass round a vast stretch of marshy ground L and later bear R into the upper reaches of the valley which is hemmed in L by the craggy ridge that culminates in Clogwyn Mawr. Continue ahead through rock and heather until the watershed is reached, whence pass through a wall and stroll downhill to the sylvan shore of Llyn Crafnant.

Clogwyn Mawr appears on the skyline L from the highest point of the path. Bear L here by a less distinct track and on reaching higher ground keep R until a cairn is encountered in thick heather. Then zigzag more steeply through the scattered crags, taking whichever way is fancied, and eventually bear L to attain the little plateau whose summit cairn is conspicuous at its western end. The vista along the Ogwen Valley suddenly bursts upon the eye and will doubtless come as a great surprise. Looking round the great arc from L to R the panorama reveals: Moel Siabod and the Llynnau Mymbyr, Moel Hebog and part of the Snowdon Group, the immense mass of the Glyders, Tryfan, Foel Goch and the Carneddau from Pen yr Ole Wen to Creigiau Gleision. There is also a bird's-eye view of Llyn Crafnant.

Plate 114 Capel Curig Post Office **Routes 27 and 28** start here

Plate 115 **Routes 27 and 28** The Path to Llyn Crafnant

Plate 116 **Route 27** Lake and path from slopes of Clogwyn Mawr

Plate 117 **Route 27** Vista of the Ogwen Valley from Clogwyn Mawr

Route 28. Creigiau Gleision. This lofty ridge is nearly three miles due north of Capel Curig and the most easterly peak in the Carneddau, over 2,000 feet in height. It is supported by a long line of broken crags, its crest is over a mile in length, and on the west its slopes fall steeply to Llyn Cowlyd. On the east, however, its gradient is easier but dappled with crags, beneath which plantations of conifers descend to the shore of Llyn Crafnant.

Follow Route 27 to Clogwyn Mawr, pass the cairn and descend steep grass on its north side. Cross a wall at its highest point and pick up the track beyond it which leads to a large sheepfold immediately at the foot of Craig Wen, a prominent rocky eminence conspicuous in the view from Clogwyn Mawr. Continue along the now less distinct track, keeping all craggy outcrops well R and on skirting the last of them the summit of Creigiau Gleision comes into view R. The cairn stands on the highest section of the long ridge and opens up extensive views to the east, in which the blue of several tarns and lakes will catch the eye. To the west, however, views of the Carneddau are restricted by Penllithrig-y-wrach on the other side of Llyn Cowlyd, but the south-western arc discloses Moel Siabod, the Glyders, Tryfan and Y Garn to advantage. Creigiau Gleision may also be reached by diverging R when Llyn Cowlyd comes into view during the ascent of Route 29.

Plate 118 Retrospect of **Route 28**

Plate 119 Last stretch of **Route 28**

Plate 120 **Route 28** – The summit of Creigiau Gleison

Plate 121 **Route 29**—The view from Tal-y-waun

Route 29. Penllithrig-y-wrach. This pointed peak is the last sentinel on the ridge descending to the south-east from the dominating peak of the group, and is a conspicuous object when seen from Capel Curig. Walk along the Holyhead road from the village and after passing Bronheulog go through a narrow gate R and follow the track past Tal-y-waun L. The direction was formerly indicated by some conspicuous power lines which have now been removed. In dry weather this was the most direct route, but as the terrain hereabouts is notoriously wet and boggy, it is better to bear L beyond the cottage, cross a low wall on the L of a deep pool and pick up a line of white-tipped posts which later veer R to join the more direct route. A leat is eventually encountered, and although the more athletic climber may spring across it and land on a muddy bank, it is advisable to turn L until a bridge appears ahead. Walk over a plank just short of it and bear R over a stile, whence the path opens up a fine prospect of Llyn Cowlyd below, enclosed by Penllithrig L and by Creigiau Gleision R. Now cross another plank L over a stream and make for a clearly marked grassy depression that terminates on the skyline, crossing several rocky outcrops *en route*. Then bear R over steep grass until the cairn surmounting Penllithrig appears on the skyline. The vast panorama round the south-western arc is revealing and includes all the familiar peaks from Moel Siabod to Carnedd Llywelyn, with below the latter a good view of Craig yr Ysfa R of the grassy Pen yr Helgi-du.

Plate 122 **Route 29**—Penllithrig-y-wrach from the Moor

[illegible] The [illegible] of Llyn Cowlyd from Route 29

Plate 124 **Route 29**—Last stretch to the summit

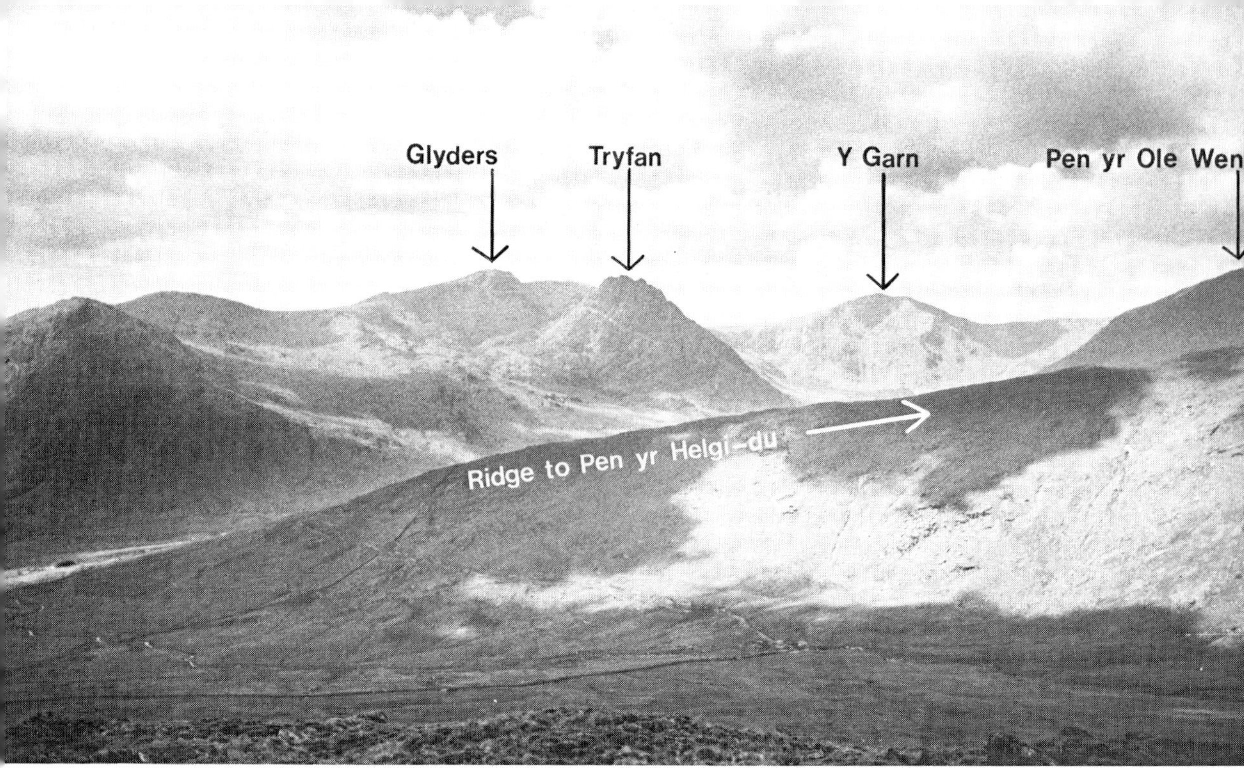

Plate 125 **Route 29** South west from Penllithrig-y-wrach

Plate 126 **Route 29**—West from Penllithrig

Route 30. Pen yr Helgi-du. This is the culminating point of the grassy ridge that takes root at Tal-y-braich, and its cairn is about two miles north of the Holyhead road. It may be conveniently approached from Helyg, by taking the side road to Tal-y-braich on the L of which is a conspicuous stile. Cross it and follow the grassy track to the north west corner of the field where a bridge spans the leat which formerly brought water down from the Afon Llugwy L to Llyn Cowlyd R. Cross the bridge, and bear R to attain the lower slopes of the broad ridge, then keep to its gradually ascending crest until the cairn is reached. The fall to the north is steep and rocky, and those wishing to extend their walk may do so by crossing the narrow ridge to Craig yr Ysfa L, or by tramping over the broader ridge to Pen llithrig-y-wrach R. The spacious views unveiled from the summit are interesting and reveal the blue of Llyn Eigiau to the north, the hills about Capel Curig to the east, Gallt yr Ogof and the wedge of Tryfan to the south, and the precipitous crags of Craig yr Ysfa, crowned by the immense summit of Carnedd Llywelyn, to the north-west. By moving over to the edge of the summit plateau L, a bird's-eye view is obtained of Ffynnon Llugwy, which occupies the floor of the wild cwm below. Pedestrians ascending this ridge *en route* for Carnedd Llywelyn may avoid the last rise to its summit by following a track L which provides an almost level course to the connecting ridge.

Route 31. Helyg, Craig yr Ysfa and Carnedd Llywelyn. This walk is one of the most interesting and revealing ascents in the Carneddau, and if the descent is made by reversing one or other of the following two routes it yields the finest circuit in this lofty group of hills, and moreover, is the most rewarding to the photographer.

Leave the A5 about a quarter of a mile to the west of Helyg and ascend the gradually rising straight new road R that ends at Ffynnon Llugwy. After passing the derelict building on the R below Pen yr Helgi-du the road bends to the L, at which

Plate 127 **Route 30**

Plate 128 **Route 30** – Craig yr Ysfa from Pen yr Helgi-du

Plate 129 **Route 31**—Helyg—The Climbers' Club Hut

point go R to join the old track rising steeply to Pen-y-Waen-wen ahead. The retrospect hereabouts is worthy of note, with Bristly Ridge and Tryfan L, and Y Garn above Llyn Ogwen R. Pass the reservoir below L and climb the twisting path that emerges on the ridge to the R of Craig yr Ysfa. Here a carpet of heather and bilberries makes a luscious foreground to the spacious view of Cwm Eigiau, with the blue of the lake shimmering in the distant north-east and L a prospect of the sharply falling crags of Craig yr Ysfa. Turn L along the ridge and scramble to the top of these cliffs by a well-worn track, but before attaining the summit glance back at the route so far ascended with Ffynnon Llugwy below. Halt awhile on the rim of Craig yr Ysfa which discloses the vast Amphitheatre, hemmed in on either side by sheer cliffs that are the treasured playground of the rock climber. Note also the undulating ridge R which displays the sharp drops on the northern flanks of both Pen Llithrig-y-wrach and Pen yr Helgi-du. Then continue the walk by ascending the long ridge that terminates on the summit of the reigning peak of the group.

The top of Carnedd Llewelyn is a vast, almost square plateau, and is a place to be avoided in mist owing to the difficulty in locating the safe ways off the peak. It supports a large cairn and its mossy surface is dappled with stones and strangely contorted groups of boulders. The panorama on a clear day is best seen by strolling round the rim of the plateau, and while it splendidly reveals the broad grassy ridges of this group trailing away to the north, with the shapely peak of Yr Elen L, it is the south-western arc that will hold the gaze. The Glyders, Snowdon and the top of Pen yr Oleu-wen lead the eye R to the long ridge of Carnedd Dafydd, with R a glimpse of the distant Rivals, Moel Elio and the beautiful sharp cone of Elidir Fawr, with still further R the sea stretching to infinity.

Plate 130 The new road to Ffynnon Llugwy—Carnedd Llywelyn in shadow. **Route 31** follows the arrow

Plate 131 **Route 31**

Plate 132 Bird's-eye view of **Route 31**

Plate 133 **Route 31** Precipices of Craig yr Ysfa

Plate 134 Craig yr Ysfa from Cwm Eigiau

Plate 135 The last ascent of **Route 31**

Plate 136 **Route 31** Summit Cairn on Carnedd Llywelyn

Plate 137 **Route 31** View from summit

Plate 138 **Route 31** Sunset from Carnedd Llywelyn

Route 32. Llyn Ogwen and Carnedd Ddafydd. Pass round the head of Llyn Ogwen and walk up to the farmhouse of Tal-y-llyn Ogwen and bear R just before reaching the gate. Then follow the wall for a short distance and cross the stile to get back onto the path above which follow the Afon Lloer into the wide mouth of the wild cwm above. Turn L and make your way through the crags at the foot of the eastern spur of Pen yr Ole Wen, and above them ascend over grass until the track L from this peak is encountered. Glance down into the cwm R and note the rough triangular shape of its lake, then follow the well-worn stony track R whose ups and downs are clearly seen as far as the summit of Carnedd Ddafydd. Before proceeding look back at the view whose skyline reveals the Glyders, Crib Goch and Snowdon above the enclosing slopes of Ffynnon Lloer, with R the tops of Y Garn, Craig Cwmsilyn and Mynydd Mawr. Then turn your steps in the direction of Carnedd Llywelyn, which now appears as an uninteresting but massive grassy hill. Descend L over the stones to a cairn and look down on the grim bastions of Black Ladders R, whose almost vertical cliffs are seldom visited by the rock climber. Pass round their craggy rim by Craig Llugwy and make your way over the broad stony ridge to the summit of the highest peak of the group.

Plate 139 The start of **Route 32**

Plate 140 Cwm Lloer seen from **Route 32**

Plate 141 **Route 32**

Plate 142 **Route 32**—Retrospect from Carnedd Ddafydd

Plate 143 Black Ladders from **Route 32**

Plate 144 Final ascents of **Routes 32 and 34**

Plate 145 **Route 33**—Pen yr Ole Wen from Ogwen Cottage

Route 33. Ogwen Cottage and Pen yr Ole Wen. The direct ascent of this lofty sentinel is by far the toughest in all Snowdonia and should only be undertaken by climbers who revel in the ascent of slippery scree that is almost everywhere overgrown with deep heather.

Leave the Cottage and walk over the bridge L. Go over the simple stone stile set in the wall R and then over the rocks to gain the steep grassy slopes ahead, whence a narrow path winds its way aloft. On reaching a rough platform the real collar work begins, and although the ascent may be continued by any of the indistinct tracks through the heather, it is easier to bear R until the edge of the slope is reached and then zig-zag L to the first top. Now climb over boulders to the second and real summit of the peak, beyond which walk along the grassy path to join Route 32 on the lip of Cwm Lloer.

The view to the south from Pen yr Ole Wen is one of the most striking in the region, because it not only discloses a remarkable prospect of the North Ridge of Tryfan, but also a superb vista right into Cwm Idwal far below. Glyder Fawr appears above Idwal Slabs, and Crib Goch, Snowdon and Crib y Ddysgl above the Devil's Kitchen. Climbers should note that photographs of these dramatic scenes are best taken in the late afternoon of a clear summer day, when the westering sun illuminates the deep cwm to perfection by the elimination of too much shadow.

Plate 146 Tryfan and Llyn Ogwen from **Route 33**

Plate 147 **Route 33**—Cwm Idwal from the summit

Plate 148 Starting point of **Route 34**

Route 34. Bethesda and Carnedd Llywelyn. This ascent begins with a long walk up a pleasant and spacious valley and concludes with a stiff climb at its head. In consequence the views are restricted until the peak is gained.

Leave the main street in the town near the Post Office and follow the uphill road to the bus stop where it forks; the right branch terminates at Gwaun-y-gwiail which stands at the broad mouth of Cwm Llafar. Follow the path with the Afon Llafar L and cross its tributary, the Afon Cenllysg, to continue beside the main stream. Ascend the path which mounts between it and the slopes of the steep ridge surmounted with crags R and with the grim cliffs of Black Ladders ahead. When Nant Ddu and Nant Fach join the Afon Llafar, follow the latter to its source beneath Carnedd Llywelyn. Then climb the steep grass to the ridge R of the peak, whence bear L for its immense summit. A longer variation takes in Yr Elen, which is reached by walking for about a mile along the path, whence bear L up its western slopes, and after passing its craggy summit keep to the narrow ridge, with steep drops L to the diminutive Ffynnon Gaseg, until the crowning peak of the group is attained.

Plate 149 Variations of **Route 34**

Plate 150 Starting point of **Route 35**

Plate 151 **Route 35**—Aber Falls

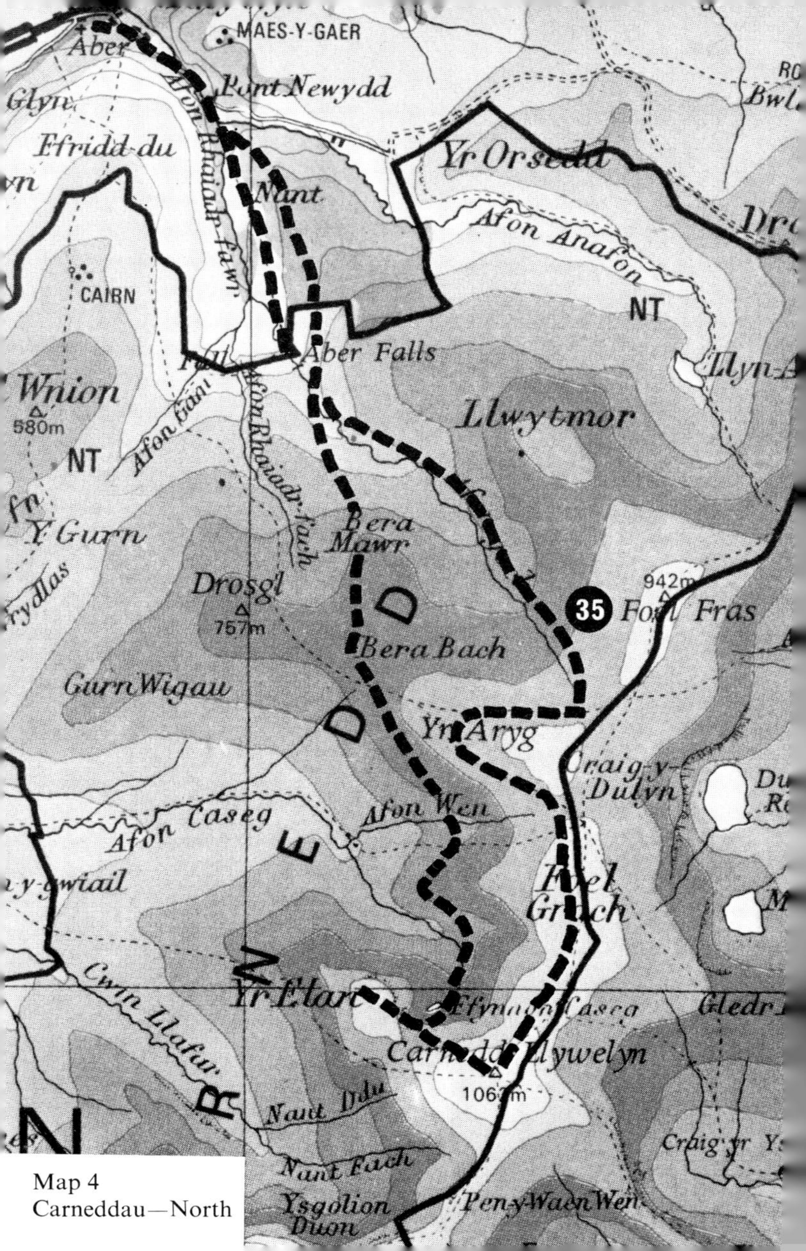

Map 4
Carneddau—North

Route 35. Aber Falls and Carnedd Llywelyn. This long walk is sometimes undertaken by climbers staying as far away as Capel Curig, and the only convenient way of doing it is to persuade someone to drive you to Aber in the morning and to pick you up at an agreed spot in the Ogwen Valley in the late afternoon. The usual starting point is Pont Newydd, with two car parks, reached from Aber by a charmingly wooded side road.

The path goes through a gate R of the bridge and is clearly marked as it winds its way beneath abundant trees for about two miles. It ends immediately opposite Aber Falls, where the Afon Goch takes a dramatic leap over some 200 feet of cliff: when the stream is in spate this splendid display should on no account be missed. This section of the valley is now Coedydd Aber National Nature Reserve. The track to Carnedd Llywelyn bears L about half a mile short of the fall and rises gradually across a vast scree slope. It then takes an exposed course on rocky slopes L, with sensational drops R to the base of the fall, and thereafter mounts over grass beside the musical cascades of the stream R. After passing a prominent sheepfold the valley widens considerably, with the craggy top of Llwytmor L, and Bera Mawr R, crowned with immense crags, whence the stream is followed as far as its sources between Foel Fras L and Yr Aryg R. Now bear R across a marshy track and climb the latter peak, whence follow the broad grassy ridge south over Goel Grach to Carnedd Llywelyn, with views R of the craggy ridge of Yr Elen below which nestles the tiny tarn of Ffynnon Caseg. Strong walkers may vary this route by leaving the Afon Goch at the sheepfold and ascending over grass to the rocky summit of Bera Mawr, but unless you are a rock climber avoid its more precipitous crags. Thence keep to the rising contours west of Yr Aryg and after crossing the spur of Foel Grach circle round Cwm Caseg and scramble up to the lofty connecting ridge of Yr Elen, which visit before attaining Carnedd Llywelyn.

Plate 152 **Route 35**—The stream below the falls

Plate 153 **Route 35**—Above the falls

The Moel Siabod Group

Moel Siabod	2,860 feet	872 metres
Moelwyn Mawr	2,527 feet	770 metres
Moelwyn Bach	2,334 feet	711 metres
Allt Fawr	2,287 feet	697 metres
Cnicht	2,265 feet	690 metres
Ysgafell Wen	2,192 feet	668 metres
Moel Druman	2,152 feet	656 metres
Moel yr Hydd	2,124 feet	647 metres

The shapely peak of Moel Siabod is the northern sentinel of a vast upland area, dappled with lakes and tarns, that sprawls in a south-westerly direction to end with the Moelwyns in the east and Cnicht in the west. It is perhaps strange that the topography of the group reveals so few mountains worthy of attention, and were it not for the graceful tapering lines of the latter which, when seen end-on from the south-west is reminiscent of the Matterhorn, it might well escape the notice of climbers. As it is, there are few who tread its isolated summit, and fewer still who scale and traverse the more distant Moelwyns. Nevertheless, there is no doubt that the group as a whole affords grand walking country, and especially that part of it centred round the attractive blue of Llyn Edno.

Since Moel Siabod overlooks Capel Curig, this is the obvious starting point for its shortest ascent, but it should be borne in mind that owing to the easy gradient of its grassy slopes it may be climbed from any side; that from the east, however, involves the crossing of much boggy ground and in consequence is the least popular approach.

To avoid raising any problems of access, climbers should keep strictly to the following routes, when going up or coming down.

Plate 154 **Route 36**—Moel Siabod from the Royal Bridge, Pont y Bala

Route 36. The Royal Bridge and Moel Siabod. Leave the village by the Royal Bridge, known locally as Pont y Bala, a wooden structure spanning the outflow of Llynnau Mymbyr, and note the splendid prospect of the Snowdon Group R. Then cross a stile giving access to the immense spruce plantations clothing the lower hillside and mount the path that winds its upward way through them, eventually to emerge from the leafy canopy with the foreshortened view of the peak on the skyline ahead. Now make your way to the top where a succession of large flat rocks deck the crest of the ridge, with sensational views L down the cliff's to Llyn y Foel, and pave the way to the cairn standing amid a chaotic collection of boulders. A variation of this route goes L above the trees and eventually reaches the crest of the north-eastern ridge of the mountain. It has the advantage of spacious views on either hand during the greater part of the ascent.

The panorama from Moel Siabod is of exceptional interest owing to its isolated position on the eastern fringe of Snowdonia, and while its extensive views round the south-western arc well disclose both near and distant objects, including Dolwyddelan Castle below, it is the western prospect of a galaxy of peaks and valleys that will rivet the gaze. The Snowdon Group first catches the eye and on the L of Lliwedd appears the sharp cone of Yr Aran, with further L Moel Hebog and its satellites. Below them there are glimpses of Llyn Dinas and Llyn Gwynant. To the R of Snowdon rise the Glyders, with both Bristly Ridge and the top of Tryfan prominent above the intervening ridge, and with further R the conspicuous sloping top of Pen yr Ole Wen leading the eye to the tremendous landscape of the Carneddau, where Carnedd Llywelyn appears above the falling craggy ridge of Gallt yr Ogof.

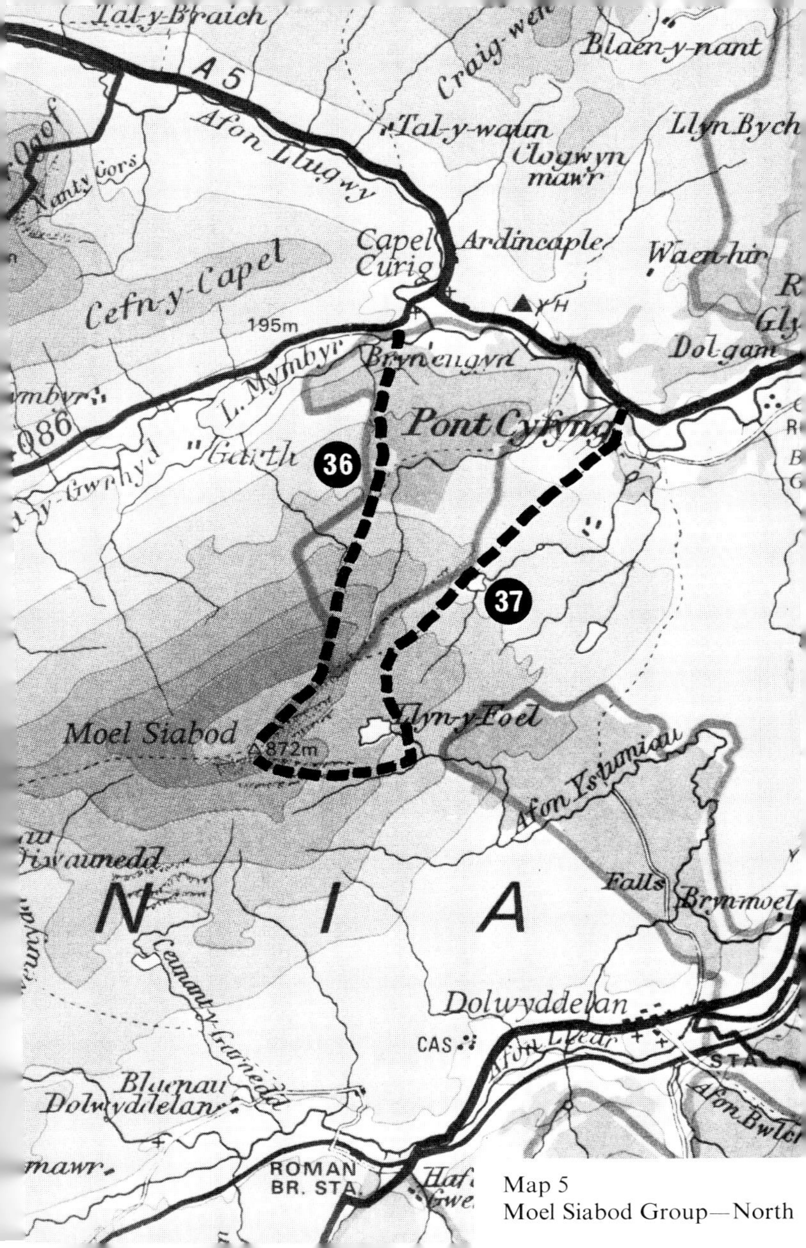

Map 5
Moel Siabod Group—North

Plate 155 Variations of **Route 36**

Plate 156 **Route 36**—Western Prospect from Moel Siabod

Route 37. Cyfyng Falls, Llyn y Foel and Moel Siabod. This is the finest and most rewarding ascent of the dominating peak of the group, because it unfolds a close view of its precipitous eastern front, an aspect that is not clearly revealed from more distant viewpoints.

Walk down the road from Capel Curig and turn R over the stone bridge spanning Cyfyng Falls. These are worthy of notice when the Afon Llugwy is in spate and a good viewpoint will be found farther down the highway. Avoid the first fork R over the bridge, but bear R at the second and ascend the old quarry road which, on emerging from the trees, passes an attractive farmhouse R. Thereafter continue along the now grassy road across the open moor, with views R of Capel Curig below and of the subsidiary top of Moel Siabod straight ahead. In wet weather the grassy road ends in very boggy ground, but it can be avoided by taking the track on the R which leads to a wire fence. Cross it and turn sharp L to pass round a rocky spur and then rejoin the path. Now go ahead past a sheet of water L until the old slate quarry buildings are reached, whence continue over a rise ahead when Llyn y Foel comes into view, hemmed in R by the rocky bastions of the peak. Walk L round the tarn and pass its outflow to gain the foot of the broken ridge rising to its summit. Climb along the edge of the crags for the view down into the wild cwm R and find a way in and out of the rocks and boulders until the cairn appears suddenly on the skyline. Climbers wishing to by-pass Llyn y Foel may go straight ahead from the wire fence and ascend slippery grass between rocky outcrops on either side. On attaining the crest, bear R for the ridge of your peak.

Plate 157 **Route 37**

Plate 158 **Route 37**—Cyfyng Falls in spate

Plate 159 Final ascent of **Route 37**

Plate 160 Cnicht from Tan-lan

Plate 161 **Route 38** Follows the course of Afon Llyn Edno

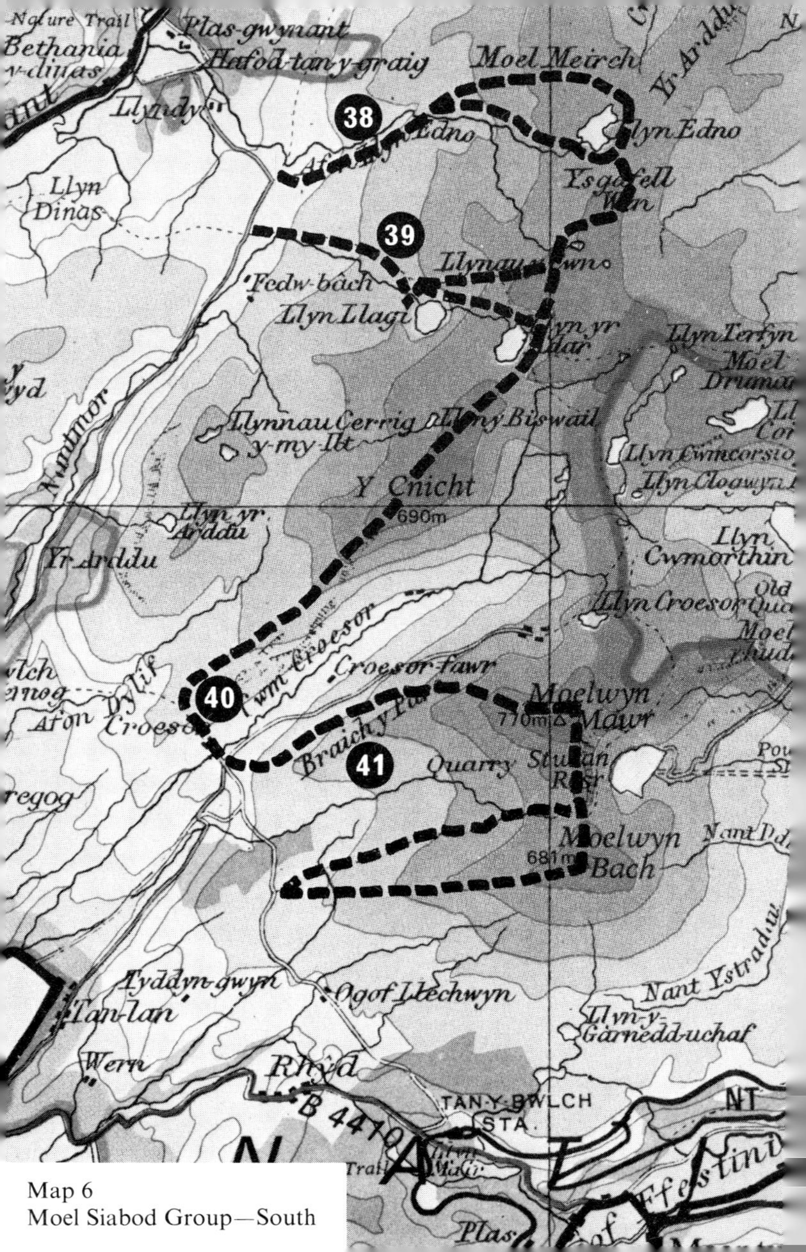

Map 6
Moel Siabod Group—South

Route 38. Cnicht by the Dog Lakes This is one of the most delightful walks in the whole group and allows plenty of time for browsing in the heather beside one or other of the lovely tarns that are passed on the way. A car is useful for getting to Nanmor, because it not only saves time which may be spent more pleasantly on the higher ground, but it also facilitates the descent of Cnicht by reversing Route 40 if the vehicle is driven round to Croesor.

Drive along the charming Vale of Gwynant and turn south for the sequestered valley of Nanmor by crossing the bridge that spans the Afon Glaslyn near Bryn y Dinas. Drive carefully up the steep and narrow side-road between stone walls, and if another vehicle is encountered one must enter a field R near the top to allow the other to pass. At its highest point the road turns sharp R near two gates and there is enough space here to park two cars. Go through the gate R and descend across pasture to reach the Afon Llyn Edno, which follow uphill all the way to its source. The immediate ascent is the steepest and roughest section of the walk, and passes through a number of romantic little gorges on the slopes of Moel Meirch L. It is worth while to look back from time to time, since the scene discloses the twisting course of the lower section of the Watkin Path, dominated by Bwlch Main and Snowdon, with L a view of Llyn Dinas and of Moel Hebog and some of its satellites.

This route is the only sure way to locate Llyn Edno, because it is cradled in a shallow basin dappled with crags, and from other directions may be difficult to find; it is said to be full of trout and the local fishermen's paradise. Halt here awhile to enjoy the fine view and note the excellent prospect of the Snowdon Horseshoe to the north-west, where Yr Wyddfa appears above Lliwedd and the ridge R encompasses Crib y Ddysgl, the Pinnacles and Crib Goch. Before leaving this secluded and enchanting spot, walk round the south shore of the lake for the vista across it of Moel Siabod whose graceful lines are especially pleasing to the eye. Extensive marshes lie to the east, and are the source of the Afon Lledr,

Plate 162 **Route 38**

Plate 163 **Route 38**—Summit ridge of Cnicht

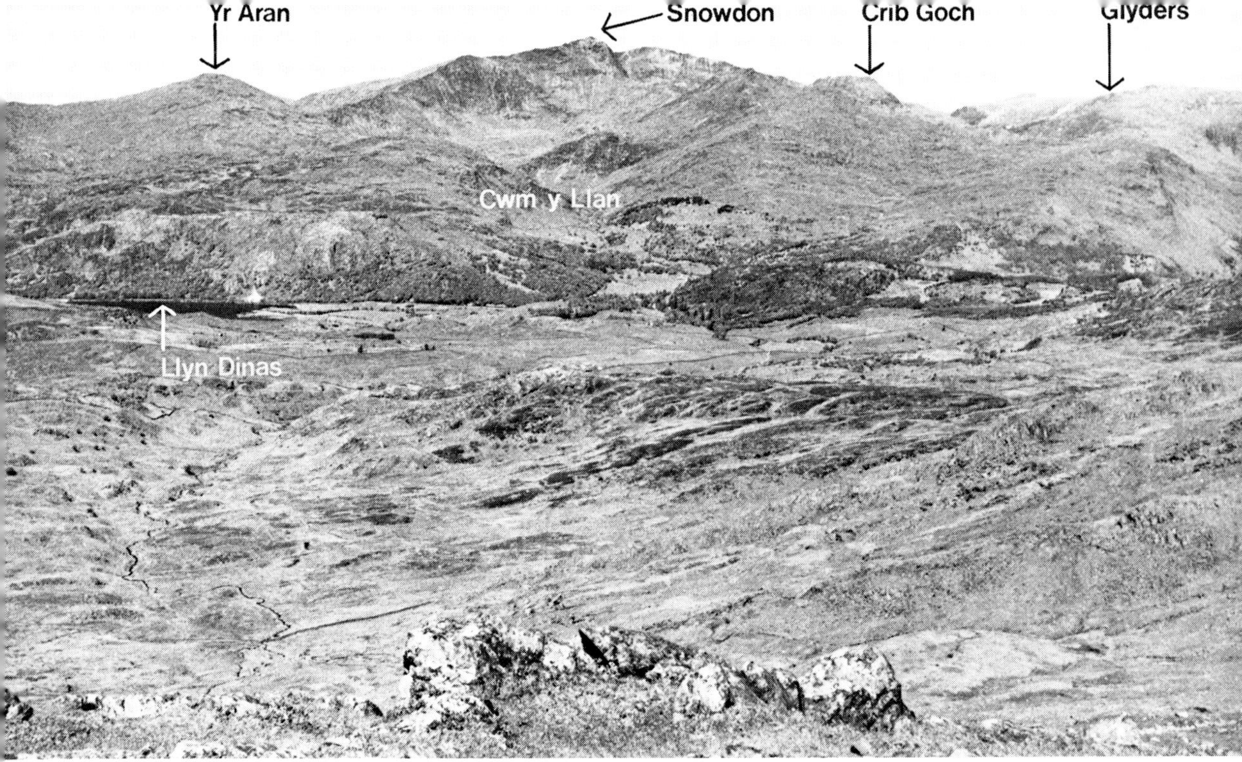

Plate 164 **Route 38**—Panorama from Cnicht

Plate 165 **Route 38**—Panorama from Cnicht

Plate 166 Route 28 Panorama from Cnicht

which, after passing Dolwyddelan with its famous castle, flows into the River Conway in the vicinity of Betws-y-coed.

Now ascend the nearby curving ridge of Ysgafell Wen which encloses these marshes, and walk south along its crest to the Dog Lakes, a collection of tiny tarns of which Llynnau Cwn R is the largest. It also unfolds another excellent view of the Horseshoe, in which, however, the precipitous eastern front of Yr Wyddfa is now clearly disclosed. Then go ahead past Llyn yr Adar R, and above Llyn y Biswail also R, to reach the base of the long summit ridge culminating in Cnicht. There are a few ups and downs on its crest and the cairn stands at its far end, overlooking Tremadoc Bay. But by following this route to the peak its most surprising and striking feature is revealed in the sudden precipitous drop into Cwm Croesor, which gives the impression of perhaps 3,000 feet whereas in fact it is only about 1,700 feet. Beyond rise the Moelwyns, whose graceful sweep is marred by unsightly and disused quarry workings. The panorama round the southern arc is extensive, with Tremadoc Bay seemingly almost at one's feet, the Harlech Dome L backed by the distant cliffs of Cadair Idris, and the Arans and Arennigs still farther L. But it is the vast panorama of Snowdonia that will hold the gaze, for this lofty and isolated peak is so placed that it reveals a chain of mountains that stretch right round the north-western arc: it is perhaps the finest coign of vantage in the whole region. The Moel Hebog group L comprises the reigning peak, the Nantlle Ridge and Mynydd Mawr; the centrally situated Snowdon group assumes graceful lines with views right into Cwm-llan where the Watkin Path is clearly seen in a limpid atmosphere; the skyline R comprises the Glyders, Penllithrig-y-wrach in the Carneddau, and ends with the nearer peak of Moel Siabod.

Note—Walkers who wish to avoid the tricky scrambling through the lower gorges of the Afon Llyn Edno should pass through the gate and follow the road on the R to the farm of Hafodydd Brithion. Beyond it they could pick up a sketchy track that ultimately joins Route 38 near a sheepfold in more open country.

Route 39. Cnicht by Llyn Llagi. This is a shorter variation of Route 38 and to reach its starting point it is necessary to drive farther along the Nanmor road and to park the car at the slate quarry where there is room for several vehicles. At the former chapel, now Blaen Nant, the track comes up from the foot of Llyn Dinas by way of the farm of Hafod Owen and continues on the other side of the road.

Follow it down to the farmhouse and pass to the L behind it to reach a gate beside the cascading stream. Continue ahead by a cairned path, with the murmuring stream R, and follow it all the way to its source in Llyn Llagi. Cross several walls *en route* and when the gradient eases off walk by the wall R across the grass to the lake. This remarkable circular sheet of water has a sombre and wild setting, and steep crags enclose its far side, broken in one place only by a perfectly straight gully that carries down the outflow from Llyn yr Adar, 600 feet above. There is an excellent camping site at its base, whence experienced climbers may tackle the gully direct. A less steep route follows a track inside the wall, which higher up is strewn with boulders and is not recommended. The easiest way is to ascend the grassy hillside to the L of the wall and turn R along the skyline. On reaching Llyn yr Adar, pass round it and join Route 38 for Cnicht.

Plate 167 Converted chapel in Nanmor—Starting point of **Route 39**

Plate 168 **Route 39** Seen from the Chapel

Plate 169 **Route 39**—Alternative ascents from Llyn Llagi

Plate 170 Route 29 The Snowdon Group from Llyn yr Adar

Route 40. Cnicht from Croesor. This ascent is just a pleasant walk and it begins at Croesor. This tiny secluded hamlet is encircled by green hills and reached by a narrow sideroad from Garreg, a village on the eastern flanks of the Glaslyn Valley. Access to the side road is gained by a sharp turn at the attractive lodge of Plas Brondanw.

Leave your vehicle in the car park on R and follow the cart track uphill on the L of the chapel until a level gap in the ridge is attained. Here the cart track bifurcates and there is also a sketchy track rising on the R. Take the R branch of the former and after passing a ruined building, cross a field and climb over a stile on the L of the gate. Then keep to the grassy track which bears R and soon attains a low break in the broad ridge. Here cross the stile on the L and go straight ahead to the foot of your mountain that now towers overhead. The several stiles and direction indicators were supplied and erected by the local Wardens Service and make an excellent contribution to safety on this most popular ascent. The ridge is reached more quickly by taking the latter course, but on attaining it you are confronted by a rocky eminence surrounded by a high stone wall. It is advisable to pass through a gap on the R, descend slightly and then attain the ridge beyond it.

Keep to the ups and downs of the grassy track which takes a direct line for the peak. The last section is steep and there are two alternative routes: that L is the more popular because it includes some easy scrambling over rock and scree; that R is easier, grassy and less sensational, but joins the other just below the cairn. The record for the ascent and descent is held by Mr. Showell Styles, who accomplished it in winter in 1 hour 18 minutes!

Plate 171 Route 40 Cnicht comes into view here

Plate 172 **Route 40**—Easy walking to the final ascent

Plate 173 **Route 40**—The steepest section of the ridge rising to Cni

Plate 174 **Route 41**—The Moelwyns from the Afon Glaslyn

Route 41. The Moelwyns from Croesor. These hills comprise three tops fairly close together and they make a fine skyline when seen from the Afon Glaslyn on the west side of the valley. Unhappily, the northern slopes of Moelwyn Mawr are spoilt by unsightly and now disused quarry workings, and of the many possible routes to the peak this ascent is chosen because it does not disclose them until the summit cairn is attained.

Leave transport in the new car park at Croesor and return to the cross roads at the entrance to the hamlet. Go straight ahead, or if coming from Garreg turn sharp R, and walk as far as the first gate on the resurfaced single-track road going over the low hills to Tal-y-bwlch. Then turn L and ascend the grassy slopes beside a stone wall, and on reaching the top of this rise the Moelwyns come into view ahead. Now bear L and cross a wall surmounted by a wire fence, and then go straight on over grass by a very indistinct track to the ridge L that rises to Moelwyn Mawr. It is clearly marked by a wire fence that runs up to a conspicuous stone tower, probably used long ago in connection with the quarry R of the peak. Finally climb the steep shaly slopes above and follow the craggy rim of the cwm L to attain the cairn at the far end of the ridge.

On a clear day the panorama round the north-western arc is of the first order and not unlike that already described from Cnicht, save that this mountain is in a direct line with Snowdon and therefore obscures the lower reaches of Cwm-y-llan. However, it has a unique feature in that immediately to the north the blue of some twelve tarns is disclosed in the sunlight and there is also a striking view of Moel yr Hydd R. Moreover, there is a more spacious prospect of the sea beyond Portmadoc and the southern arc reveals the Arennigs, the more distant Berwyns, and the great mass of the Harlech Dome, backed by the cliffs of Cadair Idris.

Now descend the grassy slopes to Craig Ysgafn, whose craggy summit is well seen from Moelwyn Mawr. Keep L over this very rough top and note the conversion of Llyn Stwlan into a reservoir far below, with Blaenau Ffestiniog beyond.

Plate 175 Croesor from **Route 41**

Plate 176 **Route 41**

Plate 177 Summit ridge of Moelwyn Mawr and **Route 40 from Route 41**

Descend the steep terminal crags of this eminence L, with steep drops also L, and follow the nail marks down to the col. Then go ahead and climb Moelwyn Bach by grass and crags L, or by easy grass slopes R, and walk over to the last cairn which opens up a superb prospect of all the peaks in Mid-Wales. The easiest way off this peak is to keep to the broad grassy ridge descending west all the way to the resurfaced road and so back to Croesor. Do not attempt to shorten the route by descending R into the vast hollow, as it is dappled with bog and extensive stretches of marshy ground, beyond which several walls and fences have to be crossed to reach the road.

Plate 178 **Route 41** Over the Moelwyns

The Moel Hebog Group

Moel Hebog	2,566 feet	783 metres
Craig Cwmsilin	2,408 feet	734 metres
Trum y Ddysgl	2,329 feet	710 metres
Garnedd Goch	2,301 feet	702 metres
Mynydd Mawr	2,290 feet	698 metres
Mynydd Drws-y-coed	2,286 feet	697 metres
Mynydd Talmignedd	2,148 feet	655 metres
Moel Lefn	2,094 feet	638 metres
Y Garn II	2,080 feet	634 metres
Moel yr Ogof	2,020 feet	610 metres

Moel Hebog completely dominates the charming village of Beddgelert, which occupies the floor of the valley at the three cross-roads, and effectively shelters it from the prevailing south-westerly winds. Its elevation is foreshortened from this near viewpoint, but its shapely stature is seen to greater advantage from the bridge over the Afon Glaslyn half a mile north of the village, and better still from the more distant head of Llyn Dinas when it is framed between the hills enclosing the lower stretches of the Vale of Gwynant. Its finest elevation, however, is revealed from Pont Cae'r-gors which spans the Afon Colwyn some two miles north on the road to Caernarvon, when its graceful tapering lines are especially attractive by late afternoon light. The ascent of this mountain makes a pleasant and easy afternoon walk, but if its immediate satellites, Moel yr Ogof and Moel Lefn, are included, then a full day is necessary for the average pedestrian.

Route 42. Beddgelert and Moel Hebog. The key to this route is the farmhouse of Cwm-cloch, which may be reached by a fingerposted path through the fields behind the Royal Goat Hotel, or by going a short distance up the Caernarvon road

Plate 179 Starting point of **Route 42** from Cwm Cloch

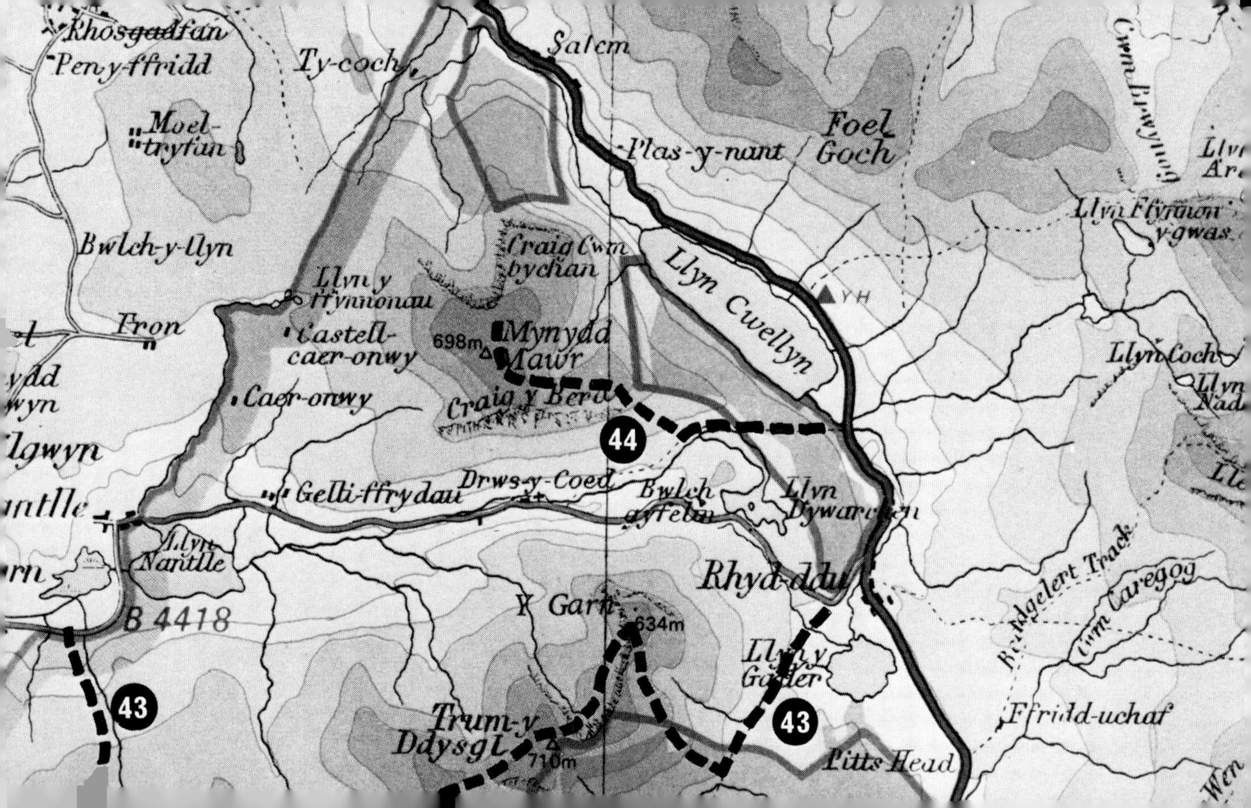
Rhosgadfan
Pen-y-ffridd
Ty-coch
Salem
Moel-tryfan
Plas-y-nant
Foel Goch
Llyn Ffynnon y-gwas
Bwlch-y-llyn
Craig Cwm bychan
Llyn Cwellyn
Llyn y Ffynnonau
YH
Fron
Castell-caer-onwy
698m
Mynydd Mawr
Llyn Coch
Caer-onwy
Craig y Bera
44
Gelli-ffrydau
Drws-y-Coed
Bwlch-y-Felin
Llyn Dywarchen
Llyn Nantlle
Rhyd-ddu
Y Garn
634m
Beddgelert Track
Cwm Caregog
B 4418
Llyn y Gader
43
Trum-y Ddysgl
710m
Ffridd-uchaf
Pitts Head

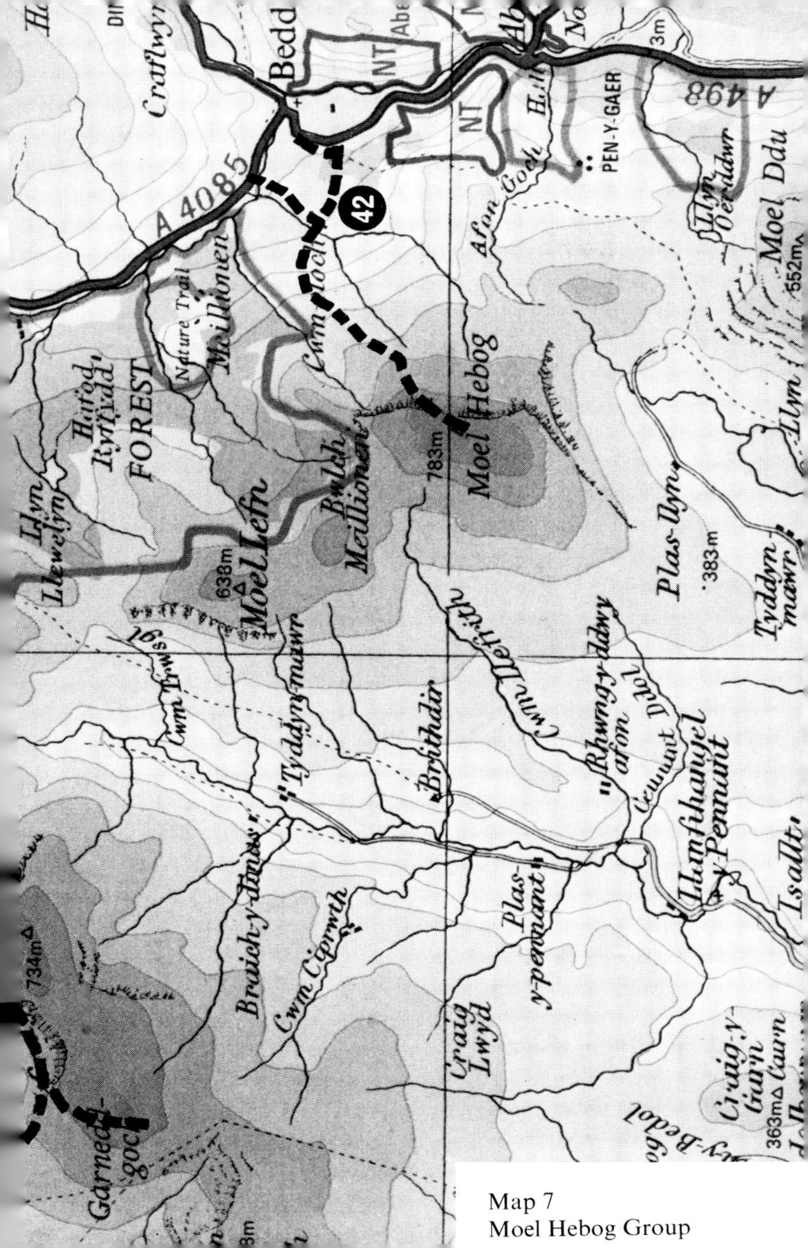

Map 7
Moel Hebog Group

and turning L over the Afon Colwyn. This bridge gives access to a by-road that passes under the long-disused Welsh Highland Railway and thence through a small pine wood to the farm. Go through a gate beside a farm building opposite and cross the usually wet pasture by a line of flat stones to a break in its far wall, beyond which a well-cairned path rises through heather and bracken. A large cairn, built on an immense boulder, will be observed high up the slope ahead and this is the key to the turning point in the route. It stands on a broad ridge in sight of the plantations and like many others on this mountain is flecked with white quartzite. It is worth while to pause here, if only to scan the scene round the northern arc, because, strange as it may seem, many of the engirdling hills look more imposing from this viewpoint than they do from the higher summit cairn. Although the Snowdon group should hold the gaze, it does not do so owing to its less interesting southern aspect, and in consequence the eye wanders R to skim along the lovely stretches of the Vale of Gwynant in which the blue of Llyn Dinas contrasts beautifully, and especially so in autumn, with its enclosing hills, to rest finally upon the lovely outline of Moel Siabod. Farther R Cnicht and the Moelwyns stretch across the skyline above the sylvan approach to the Aberglaslyn Pass, when the sharper elevation of Moelwyn Mawr from this angle will catch the eye. Now turn L at this key cairn and climb the ridge to a gate in a wall, whence a line of cairns lead uphill to the L corner of the precipitous front of the peak. Then bear R and scramble up its rocky edge to the summit.

The cairn on Moel Hebog stands some distance back from its precipitous front and thus opens up the south-western prospect of Cardigan Bay to advantage. The engirdling hills slope down gently to its shore and disclose among other eminences a fine outline of the Rivals away to the west. But to observe the northern arc it is advisable to descend slightly as Beddgelert is then disclosed over 2,000 feet below, backed by the Snowdon group and the Vale of Gwynant, a grand scene indeed.

Plate 180 Upper section of **Route 42**

Climbers wishing to extend this walk may do so by descending to the north along the ridge leading to Moel yr Ogof and continue for a further mile to Moel Lefn. This top opens up a spacious prospect of the Pennant Valley L and of the Nantlle Ridge to its R. Continue the descent to the pass below and follow the path above the plantations to Rhyd-ddu, or bear R through them for a shorter return to Beddgelert.

Climbers who know this route and might well prefer an alternative ascent, should leave their transport in the new car park at Nanmor and walk back to the bridge. Here turn L and walk about 100 metres to turn R by a path through a gate and up the zig-zags through the trees. Then pass through another gate on to the open hillside where bear R by the path for Oerddr Uchaf, whence keep R of the farm to a prominent cairn. Now proceed in a south westerly direction to join Pant Paladr trackway and follow it through a gate in the wall. Continue ahead until a cross wall is encountered, whence turn R and climb beside it to the summit of Bryn Banog. This eminence opens up a fine panorama which includes Cnicht, the Moelwyns, Cwm Pennant and Llyn Cwm y Stradlyn, together with the more distant Rivals and Cardigan Bay, all dominated in the north east by Snowdon and Lliwedd. Now descend south west to the col and climb the steep grass and scree to the summit of Moel Hebog. Should you decide to descend to Beddgelert by Route 42, leave the village by the R bank of the Afon Glaslyn and cross the bridge of the old Highland Railway, whence walk through the tunnels back to your car at Nanmor.

An exhilarating ridge walk, known as the Pennant Horseshoe, combines the traverse of the two satellites of Moel Hebog with a section of Route 43. It starts in Cwm Pennant at Pont-y-plas, rises to Moel yr Ogof and follows the ridge to Moel Lefn. Thence there is a considerable loss in height before reaching a wall ladder which gives easy access to the ascent of Trum y Ddysgl. On attaining the cairn Route 43 is followed to Garnedd Goch, whence the descent to Pont-y-plas is made by Cwm Ciprwth.

Plate 181 Final ascent of **Route 42**

Plate 182 Beddgelert from **Route 42**

Plate 183 View from **Route 42**

Route 43. The Nantlle Ridge. The walk in either direction over the hills forming this interesting and revealing ridge, which encloses Drws-y-coed Pass on the south, is doubtless the finest in this group and competes favourably with some of the better-known ones in Snowdonia. Its remote situation on the western fringe of the region makes it a prize for the connoisseur, and although I have traversed its crest from each end on several occasions I have only twice encountered other climbers on this route.

Since transport to either end of the ridge is desirable, and, moreover, as it is possible to walk there and back along its crest in a long day, it is a question of deciding at which end to begin and where to leave the vehicle, unless, of course, it can be driven from the starting point to meet the climber who only makes the one-way traverse in the day. Those who are interested in photography will find the light favourable for an east-west traverse in the morning and also for the return in the afternoon, but others who wish to engage in rock climbing on the great slab in Cwmsilin would do better to leave their transport at that end. Furthermore, not only is it easier to attain the ridge by first climbing Craig Cwmsilin, but this course avoids the longer circuitous climb to the cairn on Y Garn II. If the latter ascent is chosen, then the car should be parked in Rhyd Ddu. But if the former, then it should be driven past Llyn Nantlle Uchaf, along the first fork L to the hamlet of Tan yr Allt, and then sharp L up a narrow twisting mountain road that ends in a field beyond a farm L on the 880 feet contour, where it may be parked within easy reach of Cwmsilin.

On the assumption that the climber carries a camera, I shall describe the Nantlle Ridge from east to west, but it should be understood that some of my studies illustrating this route were in fact taken on the return walk. The two variations of the ascent of Y Garn II described in the first edition are not yet freely accessible, although those who wish to climb the peak by its north ridge, past the vertical slabs shown in Plate

Plate 184 Snowdon from the slabs of Y Garn II

Plate 185 **Route 43**—First section

Plate 186 **Route 43** /Final section

184, may possibly obtain permission from the local farmer.

Alternatively, the mountain could be climbed by first walking along the little-used path to Pennant. This leaves the road at a gate on the L about half a mile from Rhyd-ddu, at the first sharp bend to Bwlch Gylfin. Follow the wall to a farm gate, whence bear L uphill and follow the arrows in the direction of the distant plantations. But do not leave this path until you have crossed a stile, beyond which a largish boulder directs you to the L for Pennant and to the R for the ridge rising to Y Garn II. Now ascend this ridge by a sketchy track, cross another stile some way up the hill, whence climb over steep grass to the stony summit and cairn on your peak.

The extensive panorama from this lofty sentinel is justly magnificent and reveals the whole of the western aspect of the Snowdon group to perfection, with the cottages of Rhyd-ddu far below and R the cone of Yr Aran above the shimmering blue of Llyn y Gadair. To the north there is a fine view of the shattered crags of Craig y Bere on the other side of the pass, and below the rounded summit of Mynydd Mawr. To the west the first two tops surmounting the ridge are well seen and there are glimpses of the others R, with farther R Llyn Nantlle Uchaf and the sea, while to the south the broad ridge culminates in Moel Hebog.

Now turn your steps westwards and pick up the grassy track beside a stone wall L, pass the exit of a deep gully R, and start the rocky climb to the summit of Mynydd Drws-y-coed. Be careful near the top when turning L to step across a gap where rock projects above, and then keep to the edge of the summit cliffs with a big drop R. On the other side descend through crags and beyond the col follow the grassy path to the summit of Trum y Ddysgl which opens up a good backward view of the ridge and of the immense cairn on Mynydd Talmignedd. Continue down a long grass slope and make for the connecting ridge below, which has eroded so badly that the path descends L to pass this hiatus at the saddle. Then walk up to a short length of wall and go L of it to reach the conspicuous obelisk on this summit. It is so large

Plate 187 **Route 43**—Snowdon from Y Garn II

Plate 188 **Route 43**—Craig y Bere from Y Garn II

Plate 189 The trickiest section of **Route 43**

Plate 190 Ridges of **Route 43**, seen from Y Garn II

Plate 191 Hiatus on **Route 43**

that it can be seen from a great distance on a clear day and is said to have been built by quarrymen whose hobby was the erection of this pillar. The summit of Mynydd Talmignedd opens up a fine prospect of Craig Cwmsilin, with the narrow rock ridge rising to its cairn from Bwlch Drosbern, a little-used pass from Nantlle to Pennant. The distant Rivals can be seen R above the cwm, with a glimpse of one of the tarns below, and this viewpoint is one of the few from which the castles of Caernarvon, Criccieth and Harlech can be seen simultaneously. Continue the traverse by walking downhill towards the next peak on the ridge, and beyond the pass exercise care while climbing the rock ridge ahead, with steep drops L, until the cairn on Craig Cwmsilin is attained. Rest here awhile to admire the superb retrospect which unfolds the whole of the undulating ridge, backed by Snowdon. Then continue westwards and bear R over a wilderness of rocks until Cwmsilin appears below R and note the tremendous slab which is the venue of expert rock climbers, and beneath which are cradled the two glittering tarns. Descend the rim of the cwm and make for the locked gate, beyond which a grassy cart road leads direct to the car park. This is the usual terminus of the traverse, but those who wish to continue to Garnedd Goch from Craig Cwmsilin may walk over a mile of almost level stony ground, past two large cairns, whence grass and a wall lead to the final cairn on the ridge.

Plate 192 Looking back to Hiatus on **Route 43** from the Obelisk

Plate 193 Last ascent on **Route 43**

Plate 194 **Route 43** — Retrospect of the ridge from Craig Cwmsilin

Plate 105 Route 42 Optional extension and final descent

Plate 196 The Great Slab in Cwmsilin — seen from **Route 43**

Plate 197 Cwmsilin from **Route 43**

Route 44. Craig y Bere and Mynydd Mawr. Both Y Garn II and Craig y Bere are clearly visible from the road near Llyn y Gadair, and the shattered crags of the latter overhang the northern slopes of Drws-y-coed Pass. To attain them and then continue to the summit of Mynydd Mawr is an afternoon excursion which can be started conveniently from Planwydd Farm, situated on the L of the highway near the head of Llyn Cwellyn. Thence a Forestry road threads the Plantation, and opposite a building on the R a grassy break in the trees carries the power lines over the crest of the hill. This can be reached by a short cut uphill from the Farm to a gate, whence the path runs almost level to the power lines. Follow this grassy path, and on reaching open ground overlooking the Nantlle Valley turn R by the wire fence and continue along the path, crossing the stiles provided. Then ascend the steep grass of Foel Rudd which forms the prominent shoulder of your peak, and from which the retrospect of Snowdon and Llyn Cwellyn below is worth noting. Thereafter keep to the path which passes to the R of Craig y Bere as shown in Plate 200. Here you may rest awhile to observe the scene of chaos at your feet and of the ups and downs of the Nantlle Ridge on the other side of the pass, now far below. Then follow the track which rises at an easy gradient over stony ground until the cairn on Mynydd Mawr appears on the skyline. The extensive flat summit discloses Anglesey and the sea to the north, but limits the appraisal of the vast panorama of hill and valley in other directions. Snowdon is, of course, supreme, and L appear Glyder Fawr with a glimpse of Tryfan over its shoulder, then Y Garn encloses the higher tops of the Carneddau between them, while R of Snowdon the skyline encompasses both Cnicht and the Moelwyns.

An alternative descent may be made by way of Craig Cwm Bychan. On attaining its summit cairn, walk down heathery slopes in a south easterly direction to a stream which follow below the climbing face of Castell Cidwm. Here you bear R, but before reaching the shore of Llyn Cwellyn pick up the forestry ride on the R and walk along it all the way back to Planwydd Farm.

Note—At the time of writing there was no parking space near Planwydd Farm, but a car could be left either at Rhyd-ddu or near the Snowdon Ranger Youth Hostel, both of which involve a long walk to the starting point of this route.

Plate 198 Starting point of **Route 44**

Plate 199 Upper section of **Route 44**

Plate 200 **Route 44** passes to the R of Craig y Bere

Plate 201 **Route 44**—The precipices of Craig y Bere

Plate 202 **Route 44**—Prospect of Snowdon from Craig y Bere

Plate 203 The Nantlle ridge from **Route 44**

Plate 204 Mynydd Mawr from the north — Waun-fawr

Cadair Idris

Pen y Gadair	2,927 feet	892 metres
Mynydd Moel	2,804 feet	855 metres
Craig y Cau	2,500 feet	762 metres
Gau Graig	2,400 feet	731 metres
Tyrau Mawr	2,200 feet	670 metres
Craig Las	2,167 feet	660 metres
Craig Llyn	2,040 feet	622 metres
Bwlch Rhiwgwrefydd	1,838 feet	560 metres
Llyn y Gadair	1,837 feet	560 metres
Llyn y Cau	1,552 feet	473 metres
Llyn y Gafr	1,400 feet	427 metres

Cadair Idris is one of the three chief mountains of Wales and ranks second only to Snowdon in popularity. Its summit is 2,927 feet above sea level, and although forty-three feet lower than Aran Fawddwy, the highest peak in Mid-Wales, it completely dominates the district. Consisting of alternate strata of Felspathic trap and shale, it takes the form of a high ridge and extends for some eight miles between Cross Foxes on the east and Arthog on the west. Its northern front is precipitous and girt with crags which are broken in one or two places only; that of the scree slope carrying the Foxes' Path is the most noteworthy. Beneath the crags are ranges of foothills, and below these again lie the Mawddach Estuary and the town of Dolgellau. Several rugged spurs extend southwards from the ridge and give easy access to Tal-y-llyn and the Dysynni Valley, but one of them bends eastwards to form a grand rocky cwm in the bosom of which rests the stygian waters of Llyn y Cau. This magnificent scene is frowned upon by the steep, riven crags of Craig y Cau, the whole forming one of the wildest places in all Wales: it is now a National Nature Reserve.

Cadair Idris is the traditional "Chair" of Idris, a giant whom the old bardic writings represent as having been at once poet, astronomer and philosopher, and who, moreover, is alleged to have studied the stars from his rocky seat on the summit of this peak. The chair is the gigantic hollow immediately to the north of Pen y Gadair and is hemmed in on the east by the Foxes' Path, and on the west by the narrow, shattered ridge of Cyfrwy. It cradles the lonely waters of Llyn y Gadair.

The extraordinary popularity of the mountain is due in part to its accessibility and ease of ascent from all points, but more especially to the extensive panorama unfolded to the north from the entire length of its crest. This superiority of outlook is accounted for by its position in relation to the Mawddach Estuary and the valleys extending thence to Trawsfynydd Lake in the north and Bala Lake in the north-east.

Route 45. Tal-y-llyn, Cwm y Cau and Pen y Gadair. There are at least eight routes of ascent, three from each side of the ridge and one from each end of it, but the finest of them all is that from Tal-y-llyn. Walk beside this sequestered lake and continue ahead along the road to the gates of the Idris property, a distance of about two miles. Pass through the gates and enter an avenue of conifers L, which in spring is embellished by colourful rhododendron blossoms. Cross a bridge and then a stile, and turn R to ascend the eroded path that rises steeply through trees beside the stream coming down from Llyn y Cau. Pass the precipitous, rocky bluff of Ystradgwyn that is shagged with conifers R, and on emerging from the leafy canopy leave the usual path that rises through bracken L, cross the stream and then ascend its L bank to walk westwards below the long line of cliffs. There is no track and this detour involves perhaps a mile, but it has the advantage of revealing a complete frontal view of Cwm y Cau. The broken cliffs of the immense crag, together with the detached obelisk of the Pencoed Pillar L, rise above a boulder-strewn ridge that encloses the tarn hidden at its feet.

Map 8
Cadair Idris

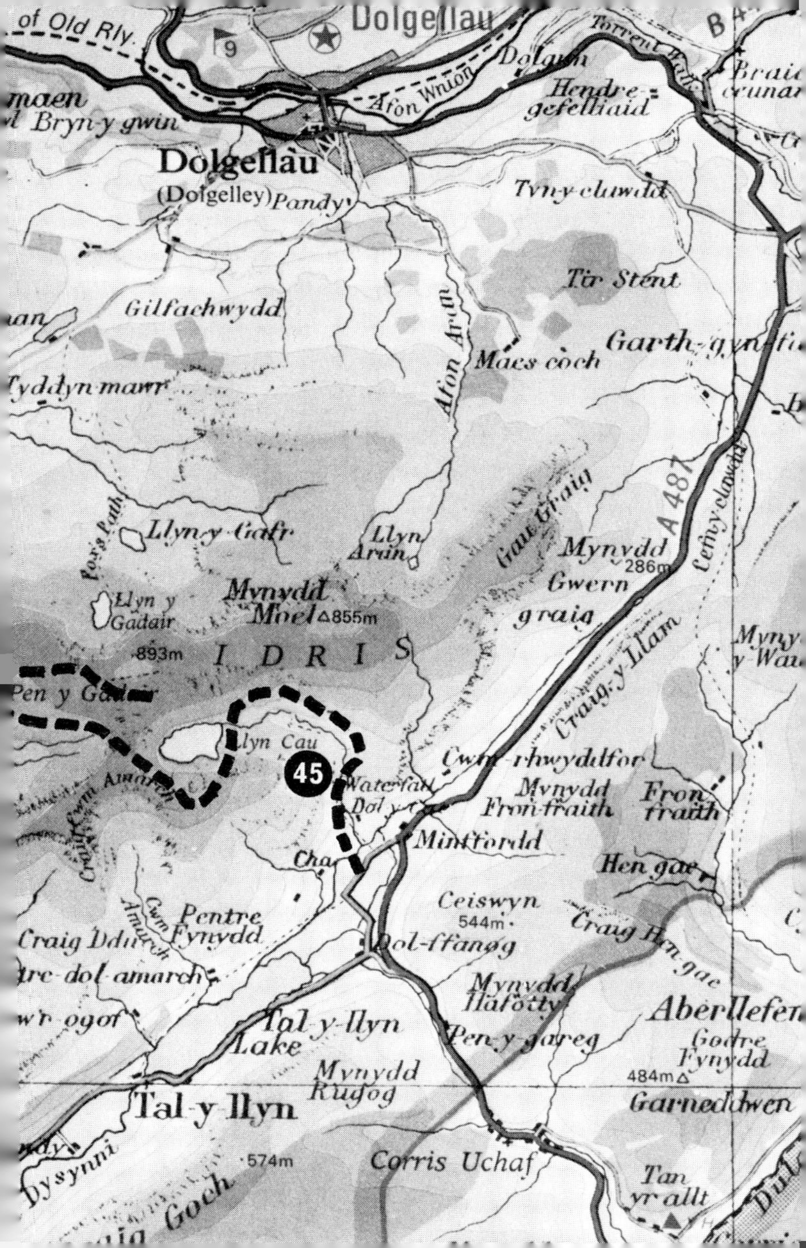

of Old Rly.
9
Dolgellau
Torrent Walk
B
Dolgun
Braich-ceunant
Afon Wnion
Hendre-gefelliaid
Bryn-y-gwin
Dolgellau
(Dolgelley)
Pandy
Tyn-y-clawdd
Tir Stent
Gilfachwydd
Garth-gynfi
Maes côch
Afon Aran
Tyddyn mawr
Gau Graig
A 487
Cefn-y-clawdd
Fox's Path
Llyn-y-Gafr
Llyn Arran
Mynydd
286m
Gwern graig
Llyn y Gadair
Mynydd Moel
855m
893m
IDRIS
Craig-y-Llam
Pen y Gadair
Llyn Cau
45
Cwm-rhwydd-for
Waterfall
Mynydd Fron-fraith
Fron fraith
Minffordd
Hen gae
Ceiswyn
544m
Pentre Fynydd
Cwm Amarch
Craig Hen-gae
Craig Ddu
Dol-ffanog
Mynydd Hafotty
Aberllefenni
Tal-y-llyn Lake
Pen-y-garreg
Godre Fynydd
Mynydd Rugog
484m
Tal-y-llyn
Garneddwen
Dysynni
574m
Corris Uchaf
Tan yr allt
Goch

Now advance over stony ground and make for the R corner of the tarn, where a conspicuous boulder is poised beside its outflow. This point unfolds a splendid near-view of Craig y Cau, whose shattered front of buttresses, gullies and grassy terraces all rise diagonally R to peter out below the skyline. On the extreme R there is a Stone Shoot that affords a quick descent to the tarn, but is not recommended in the reverse direction. The crags of this fine pyramid are not a satisfactory playground for the rock climber, but a difficult course exists on the face of the Pencoed Pillar L, which is separated from the main cliff by the fearsome Great Gully.

Continue the ascent by skirting the shore of the tarn and bear R to join the well-worn route. Climb this track which later gains the crest of the precipices enclosing the cwm to the north, and keep to its crest while enjoying the extensive views towards Tal-y-llyn L, whose shimmering blue is occasionally glimpsed through gaps in the folds of the hills. Note also the terrific cliffs of Pen y Gadair across the tarn R, and Cwm Amarch engirdled by crags L, with beyond it the long sloping ridge of Mynydd Pencoed, then walk up to the cairn on Craig y Cau.

After a well-earned rest on this breezy top, continue the walk by descending to the col that joins this subsidiary peak to the main ridge of Cadair, and note in passing the head of the Stone Shoot R already mentioned. Pen y Gadair now towers into the sky ahead and its sharp, rocky summit crowns the long ridge stretching to east and west. The track skirts the crags of this peak, but on attaining the ridge leave it and bear L along the rim of the cwm that cradles Llyn y Gadair R until the cairn at the end of Cyfrwy is reached. This is the best viewpoint for the appraisal of the tremendous terraced cliffs of Cadair and also for the long scree of the Foxes' Path L. It is, moreover, a safe place from which to observe the narrow broken ridge of Cyfrwy that falls to the conspicuous Table, once the scene of an accident to a well-known mountaineer, but since the ridge consists of loose and unreliable rock it is best left alone. Now return along the edge of the cliffs and

Plate 205 Cadair Idris from the north

climb to the summit of Pen y Gadair where there is plenty of shelter just below the cairn so that climbers can find a comfortable resting place on a cold and windy day.

When the atmosphere is clear the vast panorama of mountains, valleys, lakes and sea unfolded from this lofty perch is one of the finest in all Wales. The splendour of the northern arc discloses wide vistas of Cardigan Bay on the west, with glimpses of Barmouth at the mouth of the Mawddach Estuary, spanned by the famous bridge. The whole of Snowdonia may be seen far to the north beyond the intervening heights of the Harlech Dome, where Diffwys and the Rhinogs lead the eye to Yr Wyddfa R. The rounded summit of Rhobell Fawr is almost in line with the lonely Arennigs farther away on the open moorland, while to the north-east Bala Lake and the Arans are prominent on the extreme R. The southern arc is less spectacular and the eye is drawn to Plynlimon which may be perceived crowning the swelling moorland horizon.

Climbers who have arranged for a car to meet them at Llyn Gwernan will descend the mountain by the Foxes' Path, which leaves the ridge some little distance to the east of the summit. They will pass both Llyn y Gadair and Llyn y Gafr on the way down and obtain remarkable retrospects of the long line of precipices in the late afternoon light. Those making for the Youth Hostel at Kings will take a westerly course along the ridge and descend at the saddle of Rhiw-gwredydd, or if preferred continue to Tyrau Mawr and skirt Craig Las to reach the road. Those who wish to return to Tal-y-llyn, however, have four routes open to them: they can return the way they came, but may shorten the walk by descending the Stone Shoot at the col; they can diverge R at this point and traverse the crest of Cwm Amarch, walking thence down steep grass slopes past a little shimmering tarn direct to the lake; they can stroll eastwards along the first section of the ridge, but bear R before reaching Mynydd Moel and then go down a rather indistinct track beside a dilapidated stone wall to join the route of ascent above the

Plate 206 Tal-y-llyn and beginning of **Route 45**

trees; and they can continue along the entire length of the summit ridge to the end of Gau Graig, traversing Mynydd Moel *en route*, and thereafter descend carefully through the crags to the road near the top of the pass R. The latter is undoubtedly the finest course, with the Arans prominent on the north-eastern skyline all the way.

Walkers who prefer an easier route should park their transport in the National Car Park at Ty Nant and ascend the pony track that goes up the mountain.

Plate 207 **Route 45**

Plate 208 **Route 45**—Upper section seen from Craig y Cau

Plate 209 **Route 45**

Plate 219 Route 45 The Mawddach Estuary from Cyfrwy

Plate 211 **Route 45**—Pen y Gadair and the Foxes' path from Cyfrwy

The Harlech Dome

Y Llethr	2,475 feet	754 metres
Diffwys	2,462 feet	750 metres
Rhinog Fawr	2,362 feet	720 metres
Rhinog Fach	2,333 feet	711 metres
Moel Penolau	2,046 feet	610 metres
Craig Ddrwg	1,937 feet	590 metres
Llawllech	1,930 feet	588 metres
Moel y Blithcwm	1,804 feet	547 metres
Carreg y Saeth	1,442 feet	440 metres
Bwlch Tyddiad	1,294 feet	394 metres
Bwlch Drws Ardudwy	1,250 feet	381 metres

This is the long backbone of hills almost parallel with the coast of Mid-Wales which extends from north to south for a distance of some six miles. Moel Penolau stands like a sentinel overlooking Tremadoc Bay in the north, while Llawllech forms the southern outpost of the ridge above Barmouth Bay. Y Llethr dominates the whole chain at an altitude of 2,475 feet, but is only thirteen feet higher than its close neighbour, Diffwys. However, the two peaks which appeal more strongly to the climber are Rhinog Fawr and Rhinog Fach, because in clear weather the former reveals the whole of Snowdonia to the north, and both of them cradle a number of wildly situated tarns. Rhinog Fawr is bounded on the north by the famous Roman Steps and by the wild pass of Bwlch Tyddiad, while the two peaks are separated by the desolate pass of Bwlch Drws Ardudwy. Moreover, they are some of the most rugged hills in the country and are strewn with large boulders and scree which, to make matters worse for the climber, are literally covered with waist-high heather.

Rhinog Fawr is easily ascended from the farm at the end of

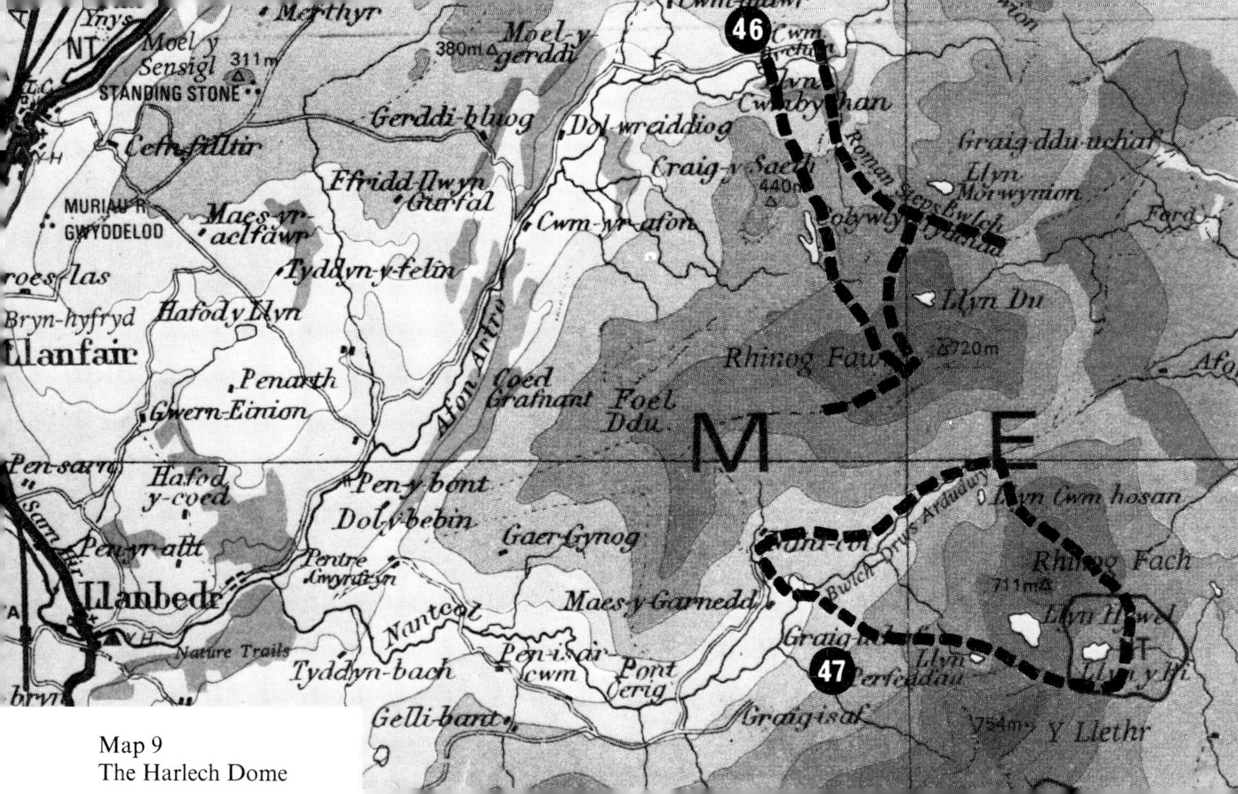

Map 9
The Harlech Dome

the narrow road beyond Llyn Cwmbychan, which may be reached from the village of Llanbedr situated on the main thoroughfare between Harlech and Barmouth. Rhinog Fach is most accessible from the farm of Maes-y-garnedd, which stands at the head of Nant Col and is the centre of the vast amphitheatre formed by the two mountains. It may also be reached from the same village by four miles of a narrow, twisting and much gated road. The following two tough routes disclose the finest scenery in the district, and include Llyn Perfeddau, Llyn Hywel and Llyn y Bi and Llyn Du, Gloywlyn and Llyn Cwmbychan, as well as the Roman Steps. *Special note*—While the narrow roads to Cwmbychan and Cwm Nantcol are negotiable by cars they should on no account be used during the holidays nor throughout the summer because they clutter up the roads and passing bays as parking areas, making the movement of essential transport by the local farmers virtually impossible. Be a sport and leave your car in Llanbedr!

Rhinog Fawr

Route 46. The Roman Steps and Rhinog Fawr The delightful sylvan Vale of Artro extends from Llanbedr to Llyn Cwmbychan a quiet little tarn overhung by the rocks of Craig y Saeth R, whence the rough hill road continues to the farm. Turn R over a bridge and follow the path through a coppice to emerge eventually on the craggy hillside. At this point it is necessary to keep a sharp look-out for the Roman Steps, which lead ultimately to Bwlch Tyddiad, because it is easy to miss their longest and best stretch as the path runs below them for some distance. It begins on the other side of a stone wall and lies immediately beneath the crags enclosing the south side of the narrow defile. According to tradition the steps were constructed by the Romans to facilitate the ascent and descent of their sentries, but they are now ascribed to mediaeval times.

Now walk along this ancient promenade to the crest of the pass and observe the featureless nature of the extensive moor

Plate 212 **Route 46**—The Roman Steps

of Trawsfynydd. Hereabouts the rugged spurs of Rhinog Fawr overhang too precipitously for their safe ascent, and it is better to go back until a weakness in the form of a steep watercourse appears in these ramparts. This is the easiest point at which to begin the toilsome ascent. Climb slowly and carefully between the large boulders almost hidden by heather for perhaps 300 feet and then edge round a big buttress to reach Llyn Du. This desolate sheet of water occupies a striking situation on the northern flanks of Rhinog Fawr and is enclosed on the south by broken precipices which extend upwards to the top of the mountain. Scale the ridge at the west corner of the tarn to eventually attain the two cairns on the summit of this peak.

When the atmosphere is clear this relatively close and lofty coign of vantage opens up a remarkable prospect of Snowdonia to the north. The Moelwyns are the nearest, with glimpses of Cnicht L and Moel Siabod R, while Moel Hebog is prominent to the north-west, with much of the Nantlle Ridge L. Between these two groups of hills Snowdon and its satellites stand supreme, and R of them and above Gallt y Wenallt there is a distant glimpse of Y Garn and Glyder Fawr. The Rivals are conspicuous to the west beyond the blue of Tremadoc Bay, and the Arennigs appear across the moorland to the north-east. Due east this aspect of the Arans is disappointing, whereas to the south and above Y Llethr the long line of cliffs supporting Cadair Idris rivet the gaze.

The quickest descent would appear to be in a direct line with the glittering blue of Gloywlyn far below, but since the intervening slopes are littered with large boulders hidden by deep heather, the walk down involves many detours and may be rather fatiguing. The lake is cradled in a shallow basin to the south-east of Craig y Saeth and, as it is a favourite with local anglers, there is a well-trodden path from its shore right down to the farm in the valley.

Plate 213 **Routes 46 and 47**—The Rhinogs from the east

Rhinog Fach

Route 47. Nantcol and Rhinog Fach. Climbers who drive from Llanbedr to Nantcol will be surprised at the number of gates that have to be opened and shut before the farm of Maes-y-garnedd is reached. The narrow and sinuous hill road threading this valley gives access to perhaps a dozen farms which may account for these several closures, but the last time I passed this way I counted them and made the number only nine, so probably others had fallen into decay.

Leave the farm and take a direct line for Y Llethr in the south-east, but keep L of its spur to reach Llyn Perfeddau which lies to the north of this mountain. It is cradled in a grassy hollow and reveals a fine view of Rhinog Fach, whose precipitous front towers into the sky to the north-east. On deserting the tarn take a direct line for it and climb a stony gully that peters out on the shore of Llyn Hywel. This tarn occupies the floor of a deep hollow between Y Llethr and Rhinog Fach, and as it is wide open to the prevailing south-westerly winds it can be a wild and boisterous place. The scene is on the grand scale and one of the most awe-inspiring in this group of hills. To the north the broken crags supporting the summit of Rhinog Fach rise literally from a sea of boulders and scree; to the south the steep ridge of Y Llethr runs up to the skyline and its sharp edge consists of gigantic slabs of rock lying end-on at an angle of forty-five degrees, while its base sinks down into the depths of the lake.

The col between the two peaks is the key to their ascent, and to attain it walk first to the south side of the tarn and then scale a gully that slants up a break in the slabs of rock. There are ample hand- and foot-holds and on reaching the skyline a wall is encountered, from which note the rippling surface of Llyn y Bi some distance below. A track runs beside this wall and gives access to most of the summits crowning this long line of hills, so if bound for Y Llethr turn R, or if for Rhinog Fach turn L where the wall terminates at the summit cairn.

The panorama unfolded from this mountain top is not

Plate 214 **Route 47** seen from the summit of Rhinog Fawr

dissimilar from that of its neighbour, save that the latter, which is twenty-nine feet higher, obscures a part of the view of Snowdonia. Begin the descent by walking along the declining summit ridge, on which the path peters out at the small cairn at its terminus, and look down the dizzy precipices overlooking Bwlch Drws Ardudwy far below. Do not attempt to descend them, but bear L and scramble carefully down the western flanks of the peak, making for the tiny pool of Llyn Cwmhosan, whence continue through boulders and heather until the pass is reached and then turn L to follow the stream down to Nantcol.

Plate 215 Nantcol—**Route 47** starts here

Plate 216 **Route 47**—Rhinog Fach from Llyn Hywel

Plate 217 **Route 47**—Slabs of Y Llethr

Plate 218 Retrospect of **Route 47**

The Arennigs

Arennig Fawr	2,800 feet	854 metres
Arennig Fach	2,264 feet	689 metres
Craig y Bychan	2,221 feet	677 metres
Moel Ymenyn	1,801 feet	549 metres
Llyn Arennig Fach	1,400 feet	426 metres
Llyn Arennig Fawr	1,326 feet	404 metres

The Arennigs are two conspicuous hills dominating the barren stretches of moorland in the northern corner of Mid-Wales. Arennig Fawr is the higher and more shapely eminence and attains an altitude of 2,800 feet above sea level, while Arennig Fach is a mere rounded hump on the heathery wilderness to the north of it, and is 2,264 feet high. Both of these mountains may be ascended without difficulty from any direction, but the latter is of little interest to the climber. The former rises immediately to the south of the old Arennig Station, eight miles from Bala and thirteen and a half from Ffestiniog. Since the station is on the 1,135-foot contour, the ascent involves only 1,665 feet of climbing.

The most direct route lies up a wide grassy hollow dappled with scree, whence the undulating ridge leads straight to the broad backbone of the summit, which falls to the south-east where it is embellished with a number of strange little peaks. This affords a favourite descent for those who traverse the mountain on the way from Arennig Station to the village of Llanwchllyn, a distance of eleven miles.

The only interesting and revealing ascent of Arennig Fawr involves a considerable detour to the south-east and skirts the shores of Llyn Arennig Fawr at a height of 1,326 feet. This lonely tarn lies immediately below a number of outcropping buttresses which are the occasional resort of the rock climber.

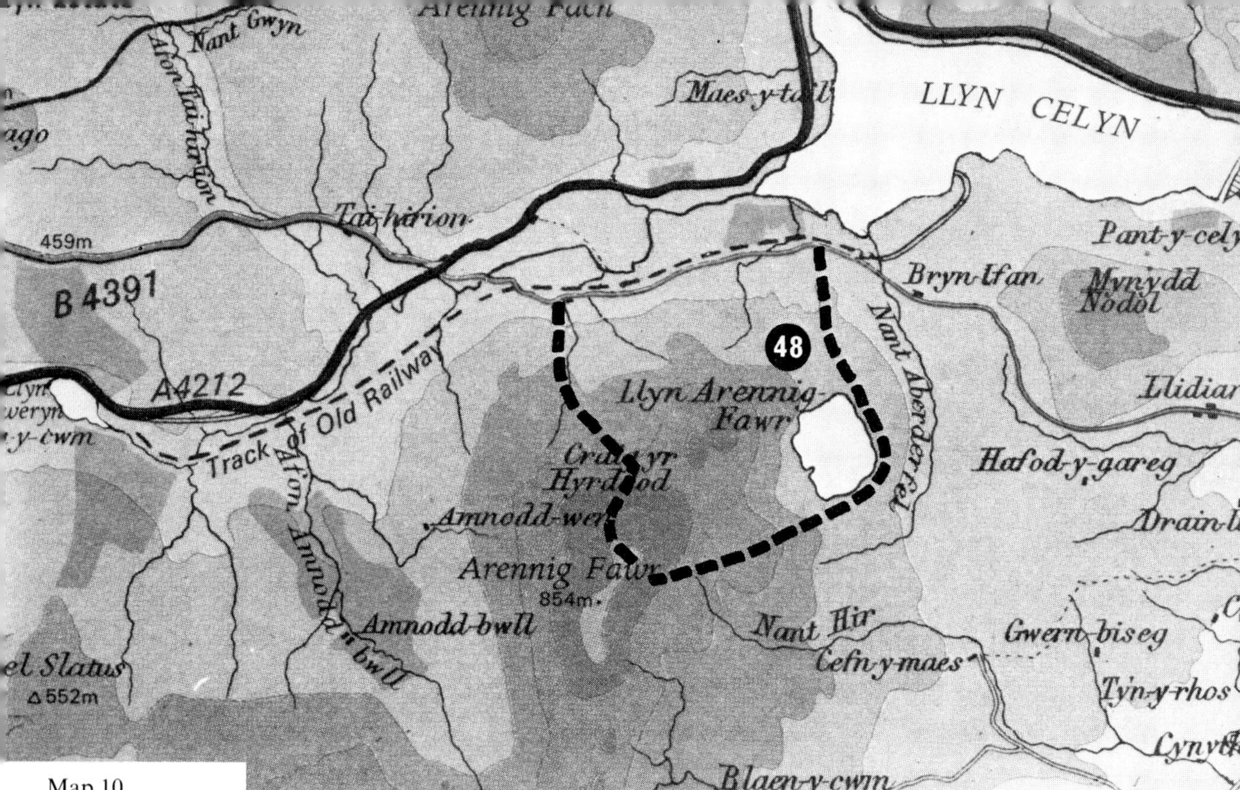
LLYN CELYN
Nant Gwyn
Afon Tai-hirion
Maes-y-tail
Tai-hirion
459m
B 4391
A4212
Track of Old Railway
Pant-y-cely
Bryn-Ifan
Mynydd Nodol
48
Llyn Arennig-Fawr
Nant Aberderfel
Llidiar
Hafod-y-gareg
Craig yr Hyrddod
Amnodd-wen
Arennig Fawr
854m
Amnodd-bwll
Afon Amnodd-bwll
el Slatus
Δ552m
Nant Hir
Cefn-y-maes
Gwern-biseg
Tyn-y-rhos
Blaen-y-cwm

Map 10

From the southern end of the lake a rough ridge leads to a grassy plateau that preludes the final slopes to the strange cairn on the summit of the mountain.

Arennig Fawr

Route 48. Bala, Llyn Arennig Fawr and Arennig Fawr. Leave Bala by the main highway to Ffestiniog, but when half a mile from the town turn L at the fork which is the old Arennig road. Pass a gate L that gives access to the open moor, where the white walls of a few tree-girt farmsteads afford some relief to the barren prospect. Continue ahead across the brown and green wilderness until the cottages clustered round the old Arennig Station come into view. During the greater part of this journey Arennig Fawr dominates the scene, but the mountain disappears behind a craggy spur on the approach to the hamlet.

Park the car near the station and walk back along the road to a corrugated iron building R, then pass through a gate on to the open moor. Follow a rather indistinct sheep track round the lower slopes of Gelli-deg R until the glimmering surface of Llyn Arennig Fawr appears ahead. Note the terraced outcrops of rock overhanging its south side, which are the occasional resort of the rock climber, but keep L round its shore. This remote tarn occupies one of the wildest and most desolate situations hereabouts and is in consequence seldom visited. Go ahead until its outflow is reached, where some piers and the dam constructed long ago confirm the conversion of the lake into a reservoir. Continue southwards and make for a rough ridge that is supported by some bold terraced buttresses. Climb the steep slopes L and on attaining its crest Arennig Fawr is revealed on the western skyline. Now walk across the grassy plateau in a direct line with the cairn and ascend the last slopes to its summit.

The first object to attract the eye on this lofty peak will be the monument erected to commemorate the death of eight gallant Americans who crashed their Flying Fortress on August 4th, 1943, their machine having collided with the rocks a few feet below the western side of the summit. Then scan the vast panorama which on a clear day is very extensive owing to the isolated position of the mountain. Snowdon dominates the numerous prominent peaks on the north-western skyline; a glimpse of Bala Lake is disclosed to the south-east and is backed by the Berwyns; the twin tops of the Arans appear almost due south, with Rhobell Fawr on R, the latter being capped by the long cliff-line of Cadair Idris; while the circle is completed in the south-west by the ridge of high hills crowned by Y Llethr.

Rest awhile to enjoy these revealing views and then begin the descent by walking due north along the broad backbone that extends below the summit. Bear R to reach the rocky terminus of Craig yr Hyrddod which opens up a bird's-eye view of Llyn Arennig Fawr below to the east, and then enter the wide grassy hollow that leads direct to the old Arennig Station.

During this descent there are also spacious views of the new reservoir in the vast Tryweryn Valley below, whose impounded water is piped to Liverpool. It is now known as Llyn Celyn.

Plate 219 Arennig Fawr from the east

Plate 220 **Route 48**—Llyn Arennig Fawr

Plate 221 **Route 48**—The Summit of Arennig Fawr

The Arans

Aran Fawddwy	2,970 feet	906 metres
Aran Benllyn	2,901 feet	884 metres
Drws Bach	2,500 feet	762 metres
Drysgol	2,397 feet	730 metres
Camddwr	2,248 feet	685 metres
Craig Cwm-du	2,246 feet	684 metres
Craig Cywarch	2,100 feet	640 metres
Craig Ty-nant	2,010 feet	612 metres
Creiglyn Dyfi	1,900 feet	579 metres
Y Gribin	1,870 feet	569 metres
Hengwm Rim	1,862 feet	567 metres
Bwlch y Groes	1,790 feet	545 metres
Llyn Lliwbran	1,550 feet	472 metres
Craig y Geifr	1,500 feet	457 metres
Moel Du	1,500 feet	457 metres

The rocky summit of Aran Fawddwy crowns the highest ridge south of Snowdonia: it attains an altitude of 2,970 feet, and is thus forty-three feet higher than Cadair Idris; sixty feet higher than Pen y Fan, the dominating peak of the Brecon Beacons; and 501 feet higher than Plynlimon. The ridge is one and a half miles in length and Aran Fawddwy stands at its southern end, the northern outpost being Aran Benllyn, which is 2,901 feet above sea level and overlooks Bala Lake.

These hills do not present an inviting aspect when viewed from the south and west and appear merely to crown a vast area of billowy moorland. If, however, Aran Benllyn is seen from Bala Lake its precipitous eastern front is disclosed, and this alone will tempt the mountaineer to climb it. On closer inspection this line of black cliffs, flecked with white quartz and seamed with gullies, will be found to support almost the full length of the ridge. The only break is at its centre, where a grassy spur extends eastwards, its lower slopes cradling the circular tarn of Creiglyn Dyfi, which is the lonely birthplace of the River Dovey.

Both of these peaks may be reached easily from any point to the north, south and west of them, but their eastern flanks are not so accessible. Those who wish to climb them from this direction may do so by walking first towards Bwlch y Groes, and then turning westwards along one of its subsidiary valleys. The most interesting ascent, however, is that of Aran Fawddwy by way of the remote hamlet of Abercywarch, which lies a mile to the north of Dinas Mawddwy. Here a narrow farm road diverges L of the highway and rises sharply between the cottages. It then threads a valley patterned with green fields and watered by the Afon Cywarch and, taking a north-westerly direction, ends at the farm of Caeperis, which is situated immediately below the frowning cliffs of Craig Cywarch. A footbridge marks the commencement of the best route to Aran Fawddwy, and ascends over grass before joining the old peat track that rises gradually for over two miles and peters out in the bogs at the foot of Drysgol. The latter is an undulating, grassy spur extending eastwards from the reigning peak, and its crest is traversed to the base of the gullied precipices that rise directly to the conspicuous cairn on its summit.

Route 49. Dinas Mawddwy and Drysgol. Leave Dinas Mawddwy by the road to Bwlch y Groes and note the sparkling cascades of the Dyfi R. On reaching Aber Cywarch turn L and on emerging from the hedgerows beyond the cottages cross the green strath to Caeperis. The farm is splendidly situated amid a circle of green hills, but on the west is overhung by the black, forbidding cliffs of Craig Cywarch. Cross the bridge and follow the path where a line of trees marks the direction of the old peat track. This rises at an easy gradient for two miles and is cushioned with springy turf and

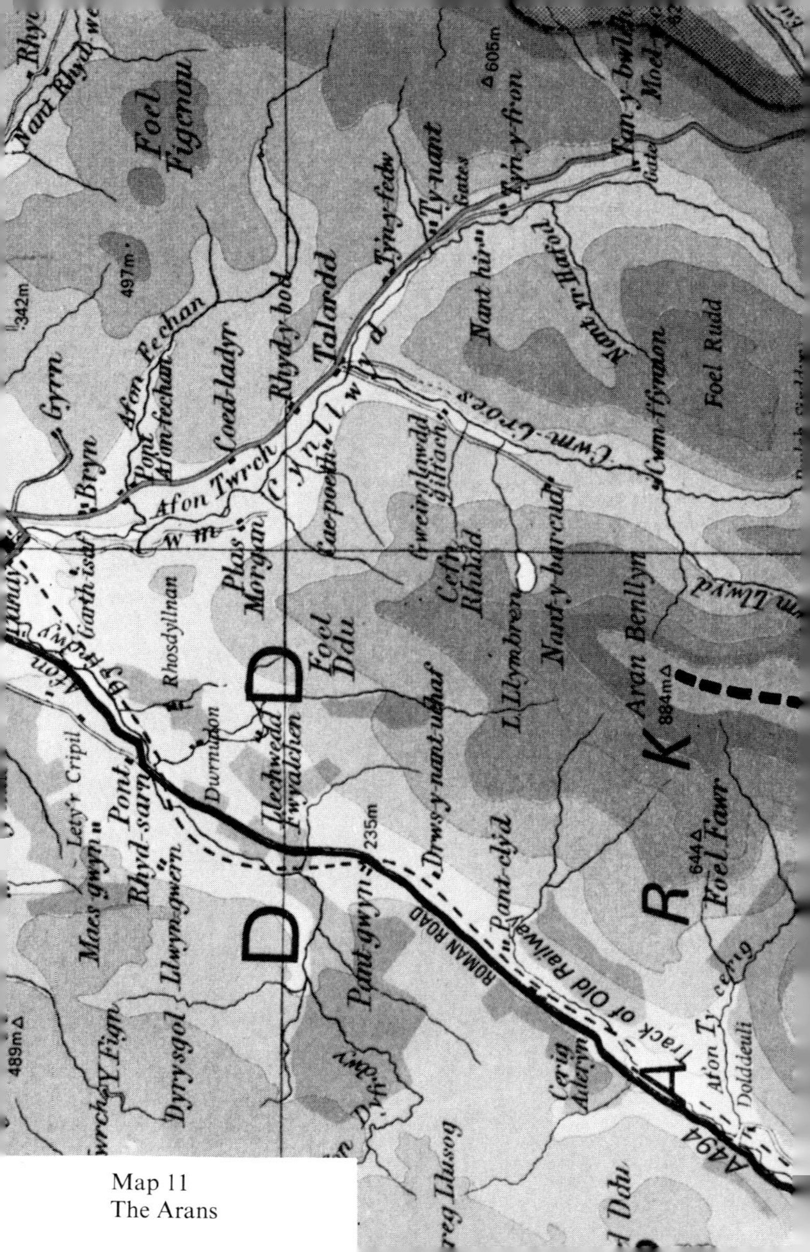

Map 11
The Arans

Aton Harnog
Cefn Glas
Llaithnant
Gallt Ceiniogau
Afon Rhiwl
Y Gadfa
Afon Cwm-ochr
Drysgol
Ogof Ddu
Nant y Cafn
Afon Dyfi
Aber-Rhiwlech
Cwm Cerddin
Cam Ddwfr
685m
Coed Cochion
Pont y Pennant
Hengwm
Pumryd
Afon Pumryd
Bryn
Cwm Llygoed
597m
Craig y Ffynnon
Llyn y Fign
779m
Craig Cywarch
Bwlch-y-Fign
655m
Llanymawddwy
Pen y-gelli
513m
Blaen Cywarch
Macnaidd
Perth-y-felin
Tyn-y-twll
Tap Mawr
Cwm Terwyn
Cwm Isaf
Bryn Mawr
Coed-cae
Tyn-y-fedw
Ceunant
612m
49
Y Gribin
479m
Plasau
Moel Lluest
NT
Bryn-Sion
Foel yr Hydd
Nant-yr-eenig
Llanerch
Moel Benddin
Afon Cywarch
Y Foel
475m
Afon Cerist
Esgair-Adda
Clywedog
Maes-Bell Dinas
Aberewarch

fringed with golden sedge. Plod along steadily and meanwhile note how the floor of Hengwm L recedes with every step until at the end of the path it is nearly 2,000 feet below. Observe also L on the other side of it the magnificent buttresses and gullies of Craig Cywarch, which have been explored by rock climbers.

Now keep to the wire fence across the maze of bog and later bear R for some outcropping rocks where a charming little pool lies on the level end of the spur. This point discloses for the first time on this ascent the shattered front of Aran Fawddwy to the west, together with the cliffs of Aran Benllyn above the grassy spur in the centre of the ridge, as well as Creiglyn Dyfi far below held firmly in the grip of the hillside by a bulge in the grassy slope.

Drysgol narrows considerably as it bends round the head of Hengwm and at one spot, where a gully falls precipitously to the south, it is so narrow that the edge has given way. This coign of vantage is a good one for the appraisal of the shattered front of Aran Fawddwy, riven with gullies and surmounted by a cairn which is clearly silhouetted against the sky. These gullies are the occasional playground of rock-climbing initiates.

Continue the walk past the cairn on Drws Bach, erected in 1961 by the RAF (SAC Michael Robert Aspin of the RAF Mountain Rescue was killed by lightning here), cross the narrow ridge and make for the L corner of the precipices. Turn R and climb the broken rocks that rise to the first cairn, or if preferred avoid them by going farther L to pick up a sheep track that mounts over grass. On attaining the crest of the ridge the reigning peak is disclosed on the skyline about half a mile to the north. Make your way through the chaotically arranged boulders and on reaching the summit cairn sit down to eat lunch and admire the spacious panorama.

A shorter alternative route begins at the gate at the hairpin bend below Bwlch y Groes on the Llanymawddwy road, follows the Llaethnant Valley and the course of the Dyfi to

Craiglyn Dyfi and ascends the grassy slopes to the saddle between Aran Benllyn and Aran Fawddwy.

Since the Arans are the most easterly peaks in Mid-Wales it follows that the most interesting views are round the western arc. Cadair Idris is seen almost end-on with the Harlech Dome R. Then come the peaks of Snowdonia and the isolated Arennigs that rise from the swelling moorland. Aran Benllyn is prominent at the end of the summit ridge, with R Creiglyn Dyfi below, beyond which rise the vast moors of the Berwyns.

Climbers who are making the traverse of this group will continue along the ridge to Aran Benllyn and then walk downhill all the way to Llanuwchllyn and eventually to Bala.

In recent years Craig Cywarch has been explored more fully by members of the Mountain Club, who, in 1960, started to build and equip a Cottage now known as Bryn Hafod, which was opened in October, 1965 and to which was added in 1974 an equipped Rescue Hut. There is ample camping space nearby and cars may be parked on the adjacent Common. In due course accommodation will be available in the Cottage for visiting mountaineers, by arrangement.

Plate 222 Craig Cywarch seen from **Route 49**

Plate 223 **Route 49**—Aran Benllyn from Drysgol

Plate 224 **Route 49**—Creiglyn Dyfi—Birthplace of the river Dovey

Plate 225 **Route 49**—The Rhinogs from Aran Fawddwy

Plate 226 **Route 49**—The Ridge to Aran Benllyn

Plynlimon

Pen Plynlimon Fawr 2,468 feet 752 metres

Plynlimon is one of the three chief mountains of Wales, the others, as already noted, being Snowdon and Cadair Idris. The summit of Pen Plynlimor Fawr is 2,468 feet above sea level, but since its environs are already lofty the mountain lacks the imposing appearance of many lesser peaks. The vast plateau extends from south-west to north-east and consists of grit and shale overlaid with coarse grass and bog; in fact satirists have described it as a "sodden weariness". However, this great dome is the source of the rivers Severn, Wye and Rheidol, and its slopes also give birth to several lesser noteworthy streams. It was Owen Glendower's lair in 1401, whence he sallied forth to harry the land.

There are two popular routes to the summit: that from Dyffryn Castell Hotel is longer and traverses three and a half miles of a broad gradually rising ridge; that from the Farm of Eisteddfa Gurig is about half the distance and threads a wild valley to an abandoned lead mine, to rise thereafter direct to the cairn on the summit. Some years ago both routes were well marked by a continuous line of stakes driven into the ground, which in mist were a sure guide, for they ran right up to the top of the mountain. But although those on the route from Eisteddfa Gurig are still in existence, those from the hotel were removed during the Second World War and have not been replaced.

Climbers who visit this region solely to ascend Plynlimon could not do better than stay at Dyffryn Castell Inn, which has ten bedrooms and a bathroom, and is right on the spot for the walk. There is a larger hotel in Ponterwyd, some two miles distant, and another at the Devil's Bridge that is four

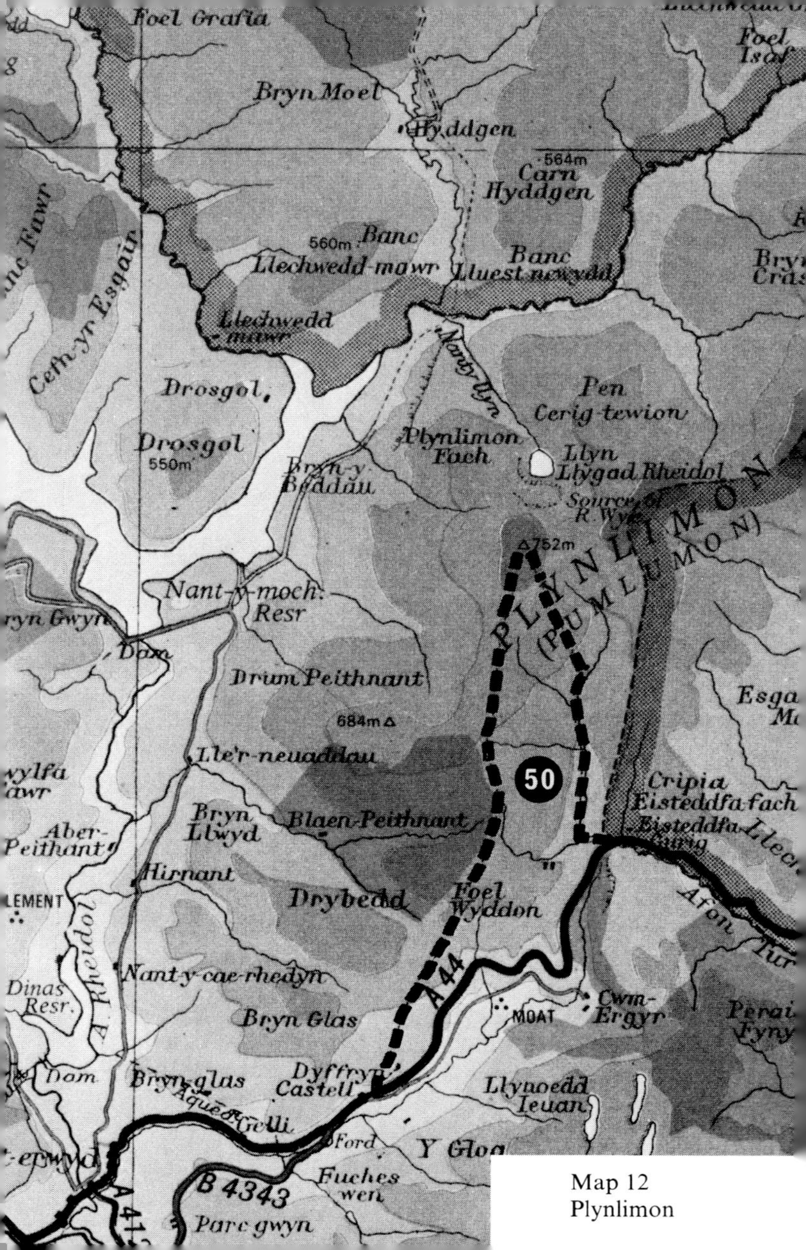

Map 12
Plynlimon

miles away. The latter has the advantage of proximity to the Rheidol Valley, a magnificently wooded basin immediately opposite, which affords charming walks for those who come to explore the district. There is accommodation at Eisteddfa Gurig, which is on the main road about three miles beyond Dyffryn Castell.

Route 50. From the Devil's Bridge. The drive to the foot of Plynlimon is pleasant and by taking the R fork at Tyn-y-ffordd the road attains the 1,005-foot contour and hereabouts opens up the only good view of the mountain. Thereafter it descends in graceful curves, eventually to merge with the main highway just short of Dyffryn Castell, where there is a car park in front of the hotel. Thence the road rises at an easy gradient along a wide, desolate valley, with the lofty grass ridge leading to the peak L, but the monotony of the landscape is relieved here and there by a few larches, which, however, disappear all too soon and by extensive spruce plantations away to the R. Eisteddfa Gurig stands at a bend on the crest of the pass and cars may be parked nearby.

Pass through two gates R of *Dyffryn Castell* and then bear L to climb the steep grassy slopes of the ridge immediately overhead. On attaining its crest bear R at an easier gradient and keep the valley in view R while ascending gradually over grass, heather and bracken for about two miles. Avoid the tremendous bogs L and always keep to the higher ground, with Plynlimon ahead slightly L until the shorter route is encountered, whence follow the stakes to its summit.

When compared with the views from other peaks in Wales, that from Plynlimon is disappointing owing to the immensity of the moorland plateau in the vicinity, which seemingly diminishes its real height. The only mountains of note in the extensive panorama are Cadair Idris and the Arans away to the north.

Eisteddfa Gurig stands on the 1,358-foot contour and the ascent to the summit of Plynlimon involves a climb of only 1,110 feet. Pass through the farmyard and follow the disused cart-track all the way to the lead mine, first beside a playful stream with chattering cascades here and there, and then R through great expanses of boggy moorland. Pick up the stakes at the lead mine and climb steadily beside them to the cairn. There is absolutely nothing to relieve the monotony of the landscape on this route: no trees to break the skyline, no colourful flowers to carpet the wayside, no birds to charm both ear and eye, just the green and brown of grass and bog. Incidentally, both routes are much pleasanter going after a dry spell.

A correspondent who knows this region intimately suggests the following alternative approaches which he says are more interesting.

Drive or walk from Ponterwyd past Nantymoch reservoir to the small holding of Brynybeddau, whence proceed up the remote valley of the Rheidol. One of three routes can then be chosen, depending on time and inclination:

1 Turn R for Llyn Llygad Rheidol and ascend through grassy crags to the summit of Plynlimon Fawr.
2 Turn up Cwm Gwarin to the top of Pen Plynlimonwstle and walk along the ridge to the dominating summit.
3 Follow the stream almost to Llyn Bugeilyn and then attain the ridge to walk back, passing the source of the River Severn en route.

Plate 227 Plynlimon from the south

Plate 228 Route 50 starts at Dyffryn Castell

Plate 229 **Route 50**—Approaching the summit of Plynlimon

Plate 230 The shorter variation of **Route 50** begins at Eisteddfa Gurig

The Black Mountains

Waun Fach	2,660 feet	811 metres
Pen y Gader Fawr	2,624 feet	800 metres
Pen y Manllwyn	2,500 feet	762 metres
Pen Allt Mawr	2,360 feet	719 metres
Pen Trumau	2,320 feet	707 metres
Twyn Tal-y-cefn	2,303 feet	701 metres
Chwarel y Fan	2,228 feet	679 metres
Pen y Beacon	2,219 feet	676 metres
Pen Gloch-y-Pibwr	2,210 feet	673 metres
Mynydd Llysiau	2,173 feet	662 metres
Pentwynglas	2,115 feet	645 metres
Black Hill	2,102 feet	640 metres

The Black Mountains cover an area of about eighty square miles to the north of Abergavenny. They consist largely of bleak, whale-back ridges running from south-east to north-west, and are dominated by the Gadair Ridge, which is crowned by Waun Fach, the highest peak in the whole group. Strangely enough all of them are about the same altitude, and rise just above the 2,000-foot contour.

Three long valleys penetrate the fastnesses of the range: the Vale of Ewyas is the longest and most beautiful and is graced by the venerable ruin of Llanthony Priory. All the valleys follow roughly parallel lines in a north-westerly direction and terminate in the shadow of a broken ridge which connects all four of the main ridges.

These ridges and valleys are excellent walking country and a variety of routes may be worked out from the new Ordnance Survey Map and in clear weather followed with little difficulty. But it is important to know some of the landmarks with certainty, owing to the very slight differences in height of a few of the peaks. This approximation in altitude is not always apparent unless they are seen from afar and a

Gwernyfed Park
Velindre or Felindre
New Co.
Tregoyd Common
Maes-torglwyd
Coed
Dyke Path
Hay Bluff
677m
Black
Pontithel
Tyle-glas
Allt Wood
Felindre Brook
Blaen-y-cwm-isaf
Pennant
Common Bychan
Bryn-ddwy-nant
Neuadd
Rhiw Wen
690m
Parc Bach
LONG CAIRNS
Rhos Fawr
Llanelieu
Talgarth
Rhiw y Fan
Darenlwyd
Afon Honddu
Cwm-Rhyd
Ellywe
Sychnant
713m
Rhos Dirion
Hosp.
Ffos-Rhys
Blaen-Bwch
Enig
Y Das
YH
The Castle
Pen-y-bryn
702m
Twyn Tal-y-cefn
Nant-y-Bwch
Pendre
Pwll-y-wrach
Grwyne-fawr
Rhyd-y-bont
Rhos
Gwrlodde
Y Grib
Pen-y Manllwyn
Grwyne-Fawr Resr.
Monastery
Capel-y-
Maes-y-ffin
510m
Tre-Walkin
4078
38

Map 13
The Black Mountains

case in point is that of the dominating Gadair Ridge where the difference in height between Waun Fach and Pen y Gadair Fawr is only thirty-six feet. When traversing the ridge this is not very clear, save perhaps from the latter top, but is quite apparent when observed from the highest parts of the Allt Mawr Ridge, over three miles to the south. When making the following ascent these features are worthy of note, and on attaining Waun Fach its summit will reveal the immensity of the range and perhaps induce the climber to make a more detailed exploration.

Route 51. The Gadair Ridge. A convenient starting point for this ascent is the sequestered hamlet of Pen y genffordd which stands at the highest point of A479, 1,060 feet, between Crickhowell and Talgarth. Climbers who approach it from the south will note the lofty ridge of Pen Allt Mawr which hems in the valley R almost all the way from Crickhowell. A reference to the map will show that Y Grib is the key to this route, and the foot of its ridge is reached by following an old farm track which passes round the north side of Castell Dinas. Advance along it for about half a mile and then take a direct line for its conspicuous spur seen on the skyline ahead. On attaining its narrow crest, which is embellished here and there by outcropping rocks, climb its sharp undulations and make for Pen y Manllwyn, a broad grassy top at the northern extremity of the Gadair Ridge. Then turn R and walk for just over a mile in a southerly direction to Waun Fach, the reigning peak of the group, which does not boast a cairn but displays only an O.S. Triangulation Station.

This lofty viewpoint unfolds an extensive panorama, in which the Brecon Beacons will draw the eye to the distant south-west, but the nearer whale-back ridges of the group are so immense that they obscure the deep valleys of the range. It also reveals the strange hump of Pen y Gadair Fawr over a mile to the south-east and its summit, crowned by a large cairn, may be reached by picking one's way carefully across the intervening boggy ground.

Plate 231 The Black Mountains from Skirrid Fawr

Plate 232 **Route 51**—The dominating remnant of Llanthony Priory

Plate 233 **Route 51**—Grib leading to Pen y Manllwyn

Plate 234 **Route 51**—Pen y Gadair and the Sugar Loaf from Waun Fach

The Brecon Beacons

Pen y Fan	2,907 feet	886 metres
Corn Du	2,863 feet	873 metres
Cribyn	2,608 feet	795 metres

Every walker or climber bent upon the exploration of this beautiful group of hills should first visit the MOUNTAIN CENTRE, which is situated about four miles to the west of Brecon and reached by a signposted road turning R off A470 near Libanus. The Centre is situated on a hill, 1,100 feet above sea level, and on the edge of an extensive stretch of mountain moorland known as Mynydd Illtud, which is separated from the Brecon Beacons by the Tarell Valley. The vistas in all directions are delightful and while admiring them refreshment may be enjoyed in the adjoining buffet. The supervisor and his assistant are usually available and willingly give information about the National Park which is admirably illustrated by an excellent display of maps, photographs and relevant literature. The Centre is undoubtedly one of the finest I have visited.

These mountains form a compact and shapely group that is situated about mid-way between the Black Mountains on the east and Fforest Fawr and Carmarthen Fan on the west. The principal summits are Pen y Fan, 2,907 feet, Corn Du, 2,863 feet, and Cribyn, 2,608 feet. Pen y Fan is the loftiest peak in South Wales and is a conspicuous object when seen from afar. The group is particularly attractive when viewed from the north, and the dominating peak assumes spectacular proportions when seen from the adjacent rib of Bryn Teg; it rises five miles to the south-west of Brecon.

The easiest and quickest way to traverse the Brecon Beacons is from the Storey Arms, which stands at a height of

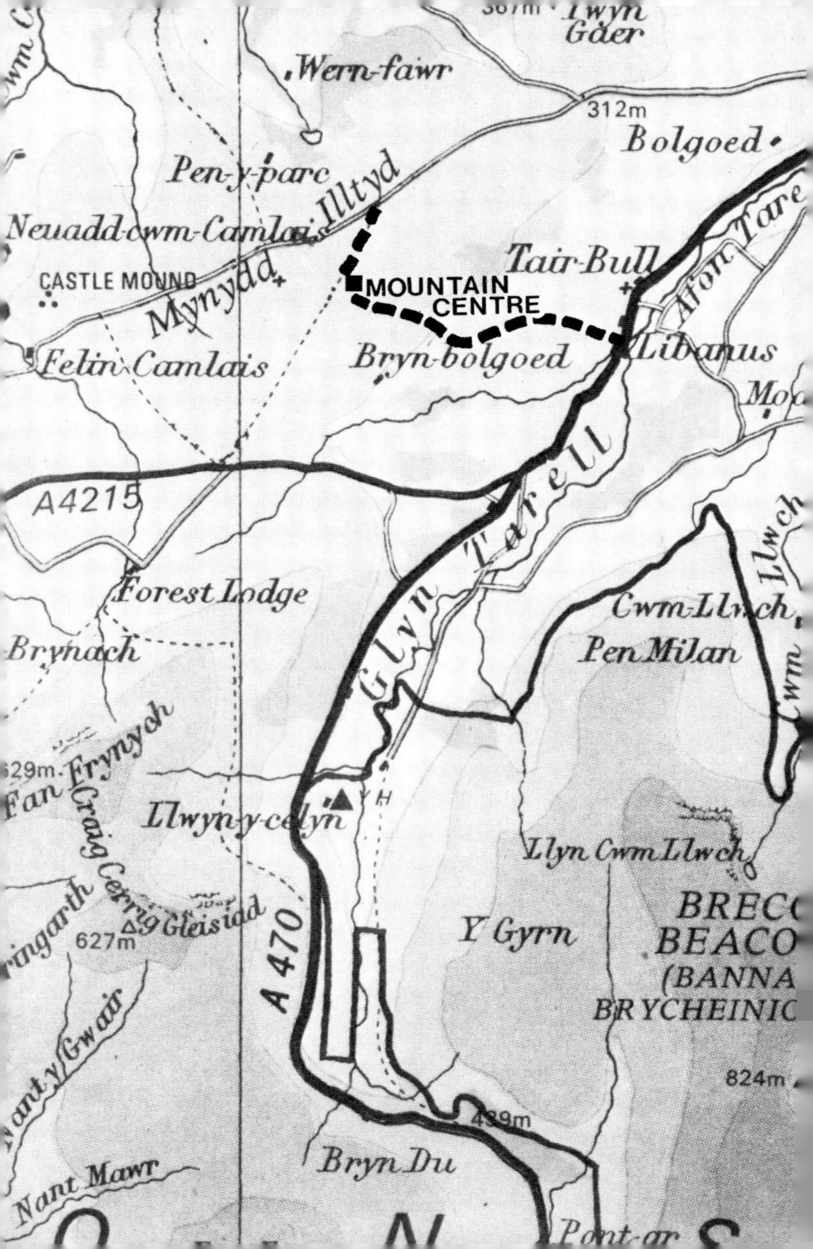

Twyn
Gaer
Wern-fawr
312m
Bolgoed
Pen-y-parc
Mynydd Illtyd
Neuadd-cwm-Camlais
CASTLE MOUND
MOUNTAIN
CENTRE
Tair-Bull
Afon Tarel
Libanus
Felin Camlais
Bryn-bolgoed
Glyn Tarell
A4215
Forest Lodge
Brynach
Cwm-Llwch
Pen Milan
Cwm Llwch
629m
Fan Frynych
Craig Cerrig Gleisiad
Llwyn-y-celyn
YH
Llyn Cwm Llwch
627m
A 470
Y Gyrn
BRECO
BEACO
(BANNA
BRYCHEINIO
824m
Nant y Gwair
439m
Bryn Du
Nant Mawr
Pont-ar

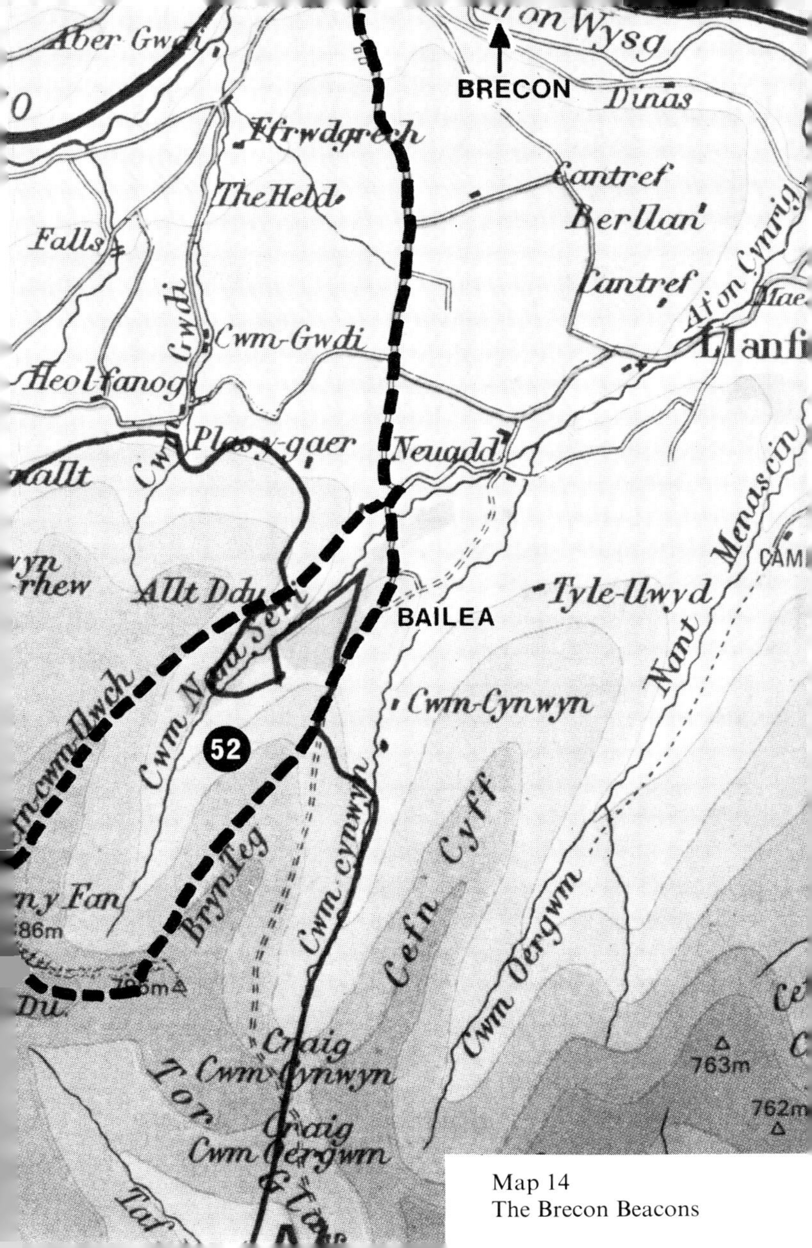

Map 14
The Brecon Beacons

1,440 feet on the crest of the pass carrying the main road south from Brecon to Merthyr Tydfil. Mere peak-baggers may be satisfied with this short ascent which involves less than 1,500 feet of climbing, but those who wish to see the real beauty of the group will miss much of it by doing so, and if they are also interested in photography and prefer, as they should, the most favourable lighting throughout, then they will follow the route described and illustrated herein.

The only snag for those without transport is that the complete circuit is a long one based upon Brecon and involves between twelve and fifteen miles of walking, depending upon such diversions as are made to toy with a camera. It is possible to drive due south from the town for three miles where the road ends with space for a few cars, and this would reduce the walking distance to perhaps seven miles. To reach this spot cross the bridge over the River Usk and then turn L off the highway at a church; the road is narrow but well surfaced and turn R at a hospital, thereafter to rise gradually in a southerly direction to end near the farm Bailea.

I first explored the Brecon Beacons in 1946 and Route 52 was then unknown, as Pen y Fan was always reached from the Storey Arms. Three years later I published a description of it in *Wanderings in Wales* and for thirty years so many climbers have followed in my footsteps that it has become the most popular route. Bryn Teg was then a bare grassy hill, with no path to the Cribyn, whereas today, after thousands of boots have climbed the Rib, it has been transformed into an easy staircase. Nevertheless, since its steepness has deterred legions of walkers, they have trodden a level path which goes off to the R and ends at the col between Cribyn and Pen y Fan, so eliminating the only section of hard going in these hills.

Note—Walkers who decide to make the ascent from the Storey Arms should bear in mind that the path leaves the main road half a mile to the south, goes through a gate, passes a cascading stream on the R and follows the line of trees on the hillside ahead. There is a commodious car park on the other side of the road, opposite the gate.

Route 52. Bailea and Pen y Fan. Proceed along the stony cartrack immediately beyond the parking space. Go through a gate and ascend the slopes of the grassy ridge, pass some small pools on its crest with the cliffs of Pen y Fan R, and take a direct line for the steep rib of Bryn Teg which culminates in the peak of Cribyn. Note the disused cart-track which contours across the slopes of Cwm Cynwyn L, and then tackle the sharp ridge ahead. This is continuously steep and the going is hard for the time being, but on reaching its summit the rewards are immense; for the full stature of Pen y Fan is now revealed in all its grandeur, its precipitous front seamed with gullies hundreds of feet long and ribbed with grass and moss to afford a picture of mountain beauty. Farther L the ground sweeps down to a little col and then rises again to the crowning peak of the range, beneath which the Afon Cynrig has its source. Now descend to the col and climb to the summit of Pen y Fan, meanwhile noting R its flat top supported by blocks of red sandstone lying end-on and poised above the innumerable layers of the same rock which alternate with successive bands of bright red earth.

The small summit plateau carries an O.S. Triangulation Station and opens up an extensive panorama in which the vast bulk of the Black Mountains appear to the east and the peaks of Fforest Fawr lead the eye to Carmarthen Fan in the west. Now continue the walk to Corn Du, whose long summit ridge is rimmed with crags R and reveals far below the circular Llyn Cwm-llwch. Then go back to Pen y Fan and descend the grassy spur of Cefn Cwm-llwch to Allt Ddu, whence bear R and walk down to the point of departure.

Plate 235 The Brecon Beacons from Penoyne Golf Course

Plate 236 The steepest ascent on **Route 52**

Plate 237 **Route 52** from Cribyn

Plate 238 **Route 52**—Corn Du from Pen y Fan

Plate 239 **Route 52**—Llyn Cwm-llwch from Corn Du

Carmarthen Fan

Bannau Brycheiniog	2,632 feet	802 metres
Bannau Sir Gaer	2,460 feet	750 metres
Bwlch y Giedd	2,400 feet	730 metres
Fan Hir	2,366 feet	721 metres

Known as the "Lost" mountain, this peak is situated twelve miles due west of the Brecon Beacons, and in plan is rather like a gigantic isosceles Triangle based on a line drawn westwards from the Gwyn Arms on A4067. It dominates sixty square miles of swelling moorland which is seamed with cascading streams, some of which disappear into the limestone, and dotted with grazing sheep. As a grassy eminence, the southern slopes of this lonely hill rise steeply at first and later at a more gentle gradient, finally to culminate in the shelter on Bannau Brycheiniog. The eastern ridge, a precipitous red escarpment, is nearly four miles in length and fringed with broken crags that drop away steeply to the moorland. It continues in an almost straight line, first to Fan Hir, and after a conspicuous break at Bwlch y Giedd, to the pointed Fan Foel. The north western rim is equally rosy and precipitous, but broken up into wild cwms. Two blue tarns grace the most northerly slopes of the mountain: to the east Llyn y Fan Fawr lies 700 feet below the summit, cradled in green hillocks; while to the west Llyn y Fan Fach lies at the foot of the frowning cliffs of Bannau Sir Gaer. There is only one hiatus in the eastern ramparts where a track, known as the Staircase, rises diagonally from the foot of the tarn to give easy access to the summit by way of Bwlch y Giedd. Each of the north western cwms carries a steep path: the first to the west of Fan Foel starts at Llanddeusant and swings round near the source of the Usk to rise in zig-zags to the ridge, but erosion has now made this ascent very arduous; the

Map 15
Carmarthen Fan

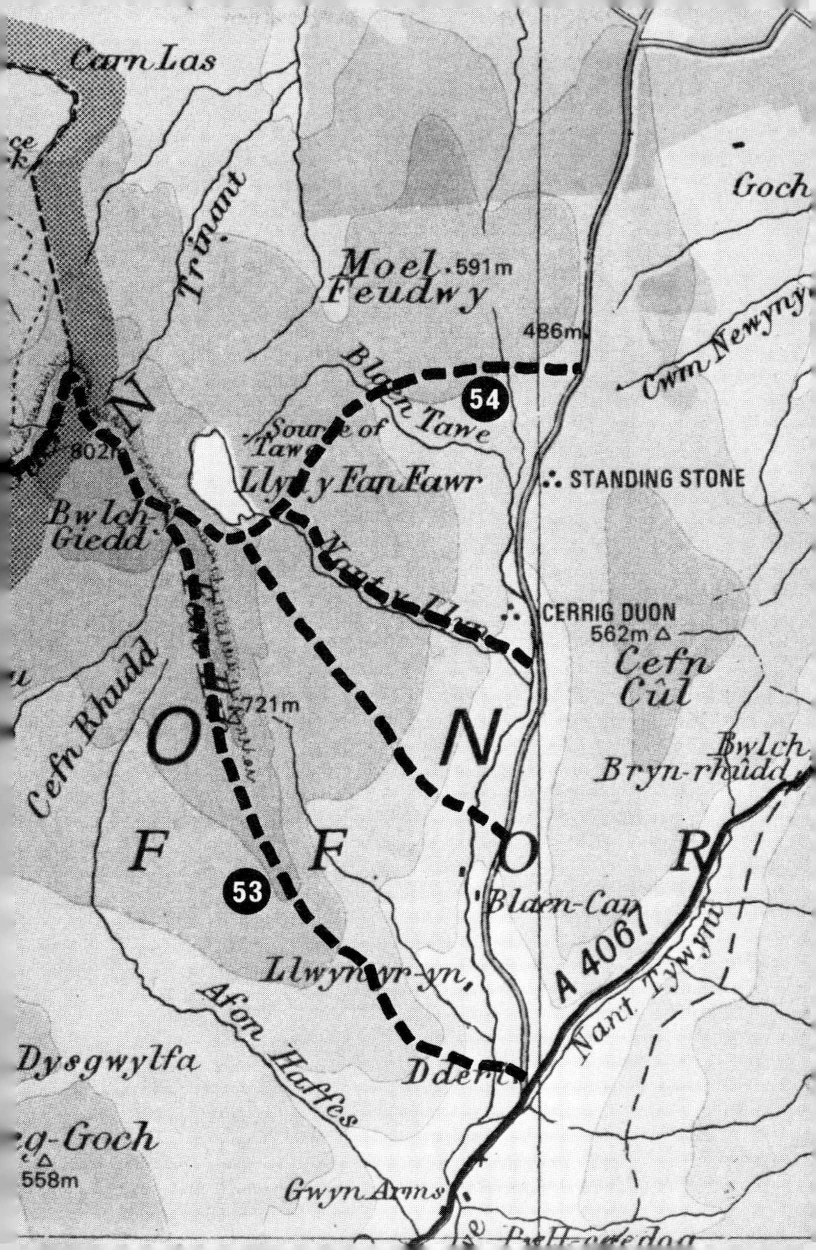

Carn Las
Trinant
Moel Feudwy
591m
486m
Goch
Cwm Newyny
Blaen Tawe
54
Source of Tawe
Llyn y Fan Fawr
STANDING STONE
802m
Bwlch-Giedd
Nant y Llyn
CERRIG DUON
562m
Cefn Cûl
Cefn Rhudd
721m
N
O
N
Bwlch Bryn-rhudd
F
F
O
R
53
Blaen-Cam
Llwyn-yr-yn
A 4067
Afon Haffes
Nant Tywynni
Dysgwylfa
Dderi
558m
Gwyn Arms

second to the east of Bannau Sir Gaer is in good condition and follows the Afon Sychlwch to its source; the third starts from the waterworks at spot height 264 m, keeps to the Afon Sawdde and passes to the R of the tarn to attain the end of the ridge.

The most comprehensive view of Carmarthen Fan is revealed from the old road running north beside the River Tawe from A4067 to Trecastle, whereas the western cwms are seen at their finest from spot height 458 m on the path from Llanddeusant to the ridge. Both viewpoints may be conveniently reached from Trecastle by taking the road south to Pont ar Hydfer where turn L for the former and keep ahead for the latter, first to Cross Inn where turn L for the church and again L for spot height 264.

Hence it will be evident from the foregoing that although Carmarthen Fan is the highest peak in South Western Wales, its situation in an often boggy and empty moorland has led to its being cold shouldered by the climber. However, this has helped to preserve it from the usual mountain scars and litter, and moreover, to retain its reputation as an unspoiled peak. Its name does not appear on the new series of maps, but the old county boundary between Breconshire and Carmarthenshire passed just to the west of its summit. It is now in Powys.

The most striking features of this mountain are all revealed near its summit; say within one mile to the east and one and a half miles to the west. The rest of its topography lacks interest and is rough sloping moorland, and anyone caught here in bad weather, where no landmarks exist, would have great difficulty in finding the exits, even with map and compass. If, therefore you decide to make the ascent, do it in clear weather.

Plate 240 Carmarthen Fan from the Standing Stone

Route 53. Gwyn Arms and Fan Hir. This mountain may be climbed by a variety of routes and that from the south is centred on Tafarn-y-Garreg where a bridge over the River Tawe, just north of the Gwyn Arms, gives access to a path which is deserted at the first farm. The hillside is ascended and by bearing R the eastern escarpment is reached and followed to the summit cairn; it is the least interesting approach and just a continuous grind over grass. The car may be parked at the Gwyn Arms now on a side road, or at the nearby church on the new road.

Route 54. Bwlch y Giedd. The key to the ascents and their alternatives from the Trecastle road is this pass, for which there are three starting points. The first begins at the cattle grid where a car may be parked on the adjacent lay-by. It makes for the conspicuous ravine opposite where the steep L bank of the cascading stream is climbed, and on attaining the more level ground it is just a walk to the tarn below the Bwlch. The second leaves the road a mile ahead and after crossing the Tawe the L bank of Nant y Llyn ends at the tarn outflow. The third is the shortest and easiest and leaves the same road just below the crest of Bwlch Cerig-duon, beside a conspicuous metal sheepfold. This is not far from the Standing Stone on the adjacent hillside and might well be described as THE STANDING STONE ROUTE. It begins with an almost level sheep track and later easy moorland slopes lead to the tarn. Now climb the Staircase from its southern end, and after passing three large cairns on the grassy slopes above it, bear R for the summit where a circular shelter provides protection from the elements on a wild day. Continue your walk to Fan Foel which is a better viewpoint because it unfolds the whole of the vast northern arc to perfection. To the east the Brecon Beacons top the distant skyline; to the north the moorland drops away to a forest of trees and a reservoir; while to the west are the cwms still to be reached. Continue your walk L along the edge of the lofty escarpment and note the magnificent elevation of Bannau Sir Gaer,

Plate 241 **Route 53**—The summit from Fan Hir

Plate 242 The summit of Bannau Brycheiniog

Plate 243 The summit and Fan Foel from Llyn y Fan Fawr

beyond which you will reach the last cwm cradling the second tarn. Return the same way or take a compass bearing on Bwlch y Giedd and cross the moor to the aforementioned cairns, and so back to your car. The time required for any of these three routes is from five to six hours of easy going and allows time to view the scenery, eat your lunch and play with your camera. There are ample parking places beside the road, together with two conveniently placed lay-bys.

Route 55. Llanddeusant. This hamlet is the starting point of the northern approach to Carmarthen Fan and follows the road going east from the church to the waterworks gate at spot height 264, from which point the view of the mountain is obscured by Twyn yr Esgair. As there is room here for only one car, it is better to drive down the rough road on the R, pass through a gate and continue L for about a mile to the Filter Beds which are situated in a conspicuous gap and where there is room for a few cars on the adjacent moorland. The path to the tarn of Llyn y Fan Fach starts at a gap in the wall on the L of the waterworks building and continues all the way to it beside the prattling Afon Sawdde. Pass to the R of the tarn and climb the end of the escarpment which follow all the way to the summit.

A possible approach from the south west is centred at Dorwen, a cottage owned by Bredon School, Tewkesbury, whence a line due north, avoiding the crags of Tyle Garw and later crossing the Afon Twrch, leads to Bannau Sir Gaer and the nearby summit.

Plate 244 **Route 54**—The diagonal path, known as the Staircase, rises to Bwlch y Giedd

Plate 245 **Route 54**—Fan Foel from Bannau Brycheiniog

Plate 246 The Brecon Beacons top the distant skyline

Plate 247 Llyn y Fan Fawr and the summit shelter from Fan Foel

Plate 248 **Route 54** continues over Bannau Sir Gaer

Plate 249 Llyn y Fan Fach from Bannau Sir Gaer

Plate 250 **Route 55**—Bannau Sir Gaer from the Filter Beds

This **Route Card** has been adopted by the Snowdonia National Park. The idea is sound and if used consistently by all climbers and walkers throughout our mountainous country it could be the means of facilitating any call for Mountain Rescue. I hope the Welsh Police will favour its use and distribute the Route Card widely wherever climbers and mountain walkers are lodged. It is, of course, most important that NO DIGRESSION is made from the stated route, otherwise in the event of an accident searchers would be unable to locate the victim.

Leave word when you go on our hills

PARC CENEDLAETHOL ERYRI
SNOWDONIA NATIONAL PARK

Names and Addresses: Home Address and Local Address	Route
Time and date of departure	Bad weather alternative
Place of Departure and registered number of vehicle (if any)	
Estimated time of return	Walking/Climbing (delete as necessary)

GO UP WELL EQUIPPED – TO COME BACK SAFELY

Please tick items carried

Emergency Food	Torch	Ice Axe
Waterproof Clothing (colour:	Whistle	Crampons
Winter Clothing (colour:	Map	Polybag
	Compass	First Aid

Please complete and leave with landlady, warden etc.
Ask landlady or warden to contact Police if you are overdue

PLEASE REPORT YOUR SAFE RETURN

Index